BASKETBALL

BY JOHN F. GRABOWSKI

Lucent Books, Inc.
San Diego, California

Titles in The History of Sports Series include:

Baseball

Basketball

Football

Golf

Hockey

Soccer

Library of Congress Cataloging-in-Publication Data

Grabowski, John F.
      Basketball / by John F. Grabowski.
          p.   cm. — (History of sports)
      Includes bibliographical references and index.
      Summary: Discusses basketball, including its origins, evolution,
the modern-day game, and famous basketball personalities.
      ISBN 1-56006-742-X
      1. Basketball—United States—History—Juvenile literature.
[1. Basketball—History.] I. Title. II. Series.
      GV885.1 .G72   2001
      796.323'0973—dc21   00-009319

Copyright © 2001 by Lucent Books, Inc.
P.O. Box 289011, San Diego, CA 92198-9011
Printed in the U.S.A.

Contents

MORE THAN MANY areas of human endeavor, sports give us the opportunity to see the possibilities in our physical selves. As participants, we all too quickly find limits in how fast we can run, how high we can jump, how far and straight we can hit a golf ball. But as spectators we can surpass those limits as we view the accomplishments of others and see how fast, how smooth, and how strong a human being can be. We marvel at the gravity-defying leaps of a Michael Jordan as he strains toward a basketball hoop or at the dribbling of a Mia Hamm as she eludes defenders on the soccer field. We shake our heads in disbelief at the talents of a young Tiger Woods hitting an approach shot to the green or the speed of a Carl Lewis as he appears to glide around an Olympic track.

These are what the sports media call "the oohs and ahhs" of sports—the stuff of highlight reels and *Sports Illustrated* covers. But to understand a sport only in the context of its most artistic modern athletes is shortsighted, for it does little justice to the accomplishments of the athlete *or* to the sport itself. Far more wise is to view a sport as a continuum—a constantly moving, evolving process. On this continuum are not only the superstars of today but the people who first played the sport, who thought about rules and strategies that would make it more challenging to play as well as a delight to watch.

Lucent Books' series *The History of Sports* provides such a continuum. Each book explores the development of a sport, from its basic roots onward, and tries to answer questions that a reader might wonder about. Who were its first players and what sorts of rules did the sport have then? What kinds of equipment were used in the beginning and what changes have taken place over the years?

Each title in *The History of Sports* also identifies key individuals in the sport's history—people whose leadership or skills have made a difference in the way the sport is played today. Included will be the easily recognized names, the Mia Hamms and the Sammy Sosas, the Wilt Chamberlains and the Wilma Rudolphs. But there are also the names of past greats, people like baseball's King Kelly, soccer's Sir Stanley Matthews, and basketball's Hank Luisetti—who may be less familiar today, but were as synonymous with their sports at one time as the "oohs and ahhs" players of today.

Finally, the series looks at the aspects of a sport that are particularly important in its current point on the continuum. Baseball today is better understood knowing about salary caps and union negotiators. One cannot truly know modern soccer without knowing about the specter of fan violence at matches. And learning about the role of instant replay is critical to a thorough understanding of today's professional football games. In viewing a sport as a continuum, the strides that have been made along the way are that much more admirable. It is a richer view, and one that shows how yesterday's limits have been surpassed—and how the limits of today are the possibilities of athletes in the future.

A Worldwide Mania

WHEN JAMES NAISMITH invented the sport of basketball in 1891, his whole purpose for doing so was to come up with a new activity for a rowdy class of young men. He could not possibly have imagined, even in his wildest dreams, that his creation would one day become one of the most popular sports in the world.

Basketball is probably played in more countries than any other team sport. Although baseball is popular in Latin America, Japan, and Australia, and American football and soccer are favorites in Europe, more than 175 nations currently boast of national basketball federations. What is the reason for this surge in basketball's popularity around the globe?

One obvious explanation is the simplicity of the game itself. Despite the number of changes that have taken place over the years, basketball still has far fewer rules than either baseball or football. A newcomer to the game can pick up the fundamentals in a far shorter time than a baseball or football novice. Despite this simplicity, however, the game still requires a great deal of time and practice in order to become proficient at it.

Compared with other sports, basketball's equipment is also much simpler, requiring only a ball and a hoop. No special gloves or clothing is required, although sneakers are the preferred foot covering. Cost, therefore, is minimal. Bats, pads, or helmets are necessities in the other two major sports, even at the beginner level.

Basketball can be played indoors all year-round no matter what the weather outside may be. "The ground," wrote Naismith, "may be the gymnasium floor cleared of apparatus . . . though it could be played in the open air at a picnic, etc."[1] It can be played in any kind of weather, in any season of the year.

The space required to play the game is minimal. Three full-sized basketball courts take up less area than a regulation football field or baseball diamond. And as anyone who has played three-on-three games in a driveway knows, a full-sized court is not even a necessity. Space is the main reason why basketball has come to be known as the "city game." Baseball and football are not as accessible to those who live in urban areas.

The game is also much more popular among girls and women. Whereas many women may enjoy watching baseball or football, many more actually play basketball, particularly at the high school and college level. Beyond that, no other team game can boast of a thriving professional women's league.

Fans at a basketball game are closer to the action than in baseball or football. Likewise, the players do not wear hats or helmets, so their faces are more visible. Spectators can identify the range of emotions experienced by the players as the game progresses, empathizing with them through both peaks and valleys. This can give them a closer attachment to the game than in other sports.

Basketball's popularity, however, is probably due to the number of people required to play a game. A regulation game of football requires eleven players on each side, and baseball, nine. Five players constitute a team in basketball, and if ten players are not available, a game can be played by eight, six, four, or even just two persons. Basketball, in fact, is probably the only team sport that can be enjoyed by a single person, play-

Many women play basketball, particularly at the high school and college level.

ing alone, with no opponent at all.

Whatever the reason may be, it is certain that interest in basketball around the world has never been higher than it is today. Through worldwide marketing, players such as Michael Jordan are known in every corner of the planet.

For many, baseball is too slow, football too structured, and hockey too low-scoring.

Basketball, with its improvisational moves and high-scoring action, has more appeal to individuals caught up in our fast-paced, modern world. James Naismith's game, born in Springfield, Massachusetts, more than a century ago, is arguably the ideal sport for the twenty-first century. Millions of fans around the world would most certainly agree.

CHAPTER 1

From Humble Beginnings

THREE OF THE four major team sports played in America today evolved over a period of time from various other pastimes. Baseball sprang up as an offshoot of the British games of rounders and town ball. Football is derived from rugby, another British sport. Hockey evolved from a game called *hoquet*, which was played by North American Indians.

Of the four sports, only basketball can point to an exact time and place for its birth. It emerged from the mind of a single man, who wrote down the rules for his invention more than a hundred years ago. That man was James Naismith.

Needed: A New Activity

Naismith was a Canadian raised in the rural Ontario village of Bennie's Corners. He had been a superior athlete as a student at McGill University in Montreal. Twice, he was named the school's top all-around athlete. In addition to competing in soccer, rugby, and track, he also played lacrosse professionally with the Montreal Shamrocks.

Resolved to entering the ministry, Naismith studied theology at Presbyterian College after his graduation. In 1890, he continued his education as a student at the International Young Men's Christian Association Training School—now Springfield College—in Springfield, Massachusetts, where he studied physical education. The next year, he was invited to stay as an instructor. He accepted the offer, feeling that this would allow him to combine two of his main fields of interest, the ministry and athletics.

While at Springfield, Naismith was assigned a group of eighteen future Young Men's Christian Association (YMCA) general secretaries. The young men in the class took part in football in the fall and in baseball in the spring. The winter months, however, posed a problem: Calisthenics, marching, and gymnastics were the major activities, and the students quickly became bored. As Naismith put it, "Those boys simply would not play drop the handkerchief."[2]

Two previous instructors had failed in their efforts at controlling the class. At a faculty meeting, Naismith happened to voice the opinion that it should be possible to invent a new game that would be "interesting, easy to learn, and easy to play in the winter and by artificial light."[3] Anxious for the matter to be settled, Luther Halsey Gulick, the physical education department's chairman, assigned Naismith the job of coming up with just such an activity, and gave him two weeks to do so.

Developing a New Game

At first Naismith tried indoor versions of lacrosse, soccer, and rugby, all without success. He even tried a new game, called "battle-ball," again without success. He then decided to approach the task systematically and logically. He examined other sports, breaking up each into its component parts. He applied this research in the development of a new game. "Dr. Gulick had reminded me on one occasion," recalled Naismith, "that there is nothing new under the sun. What appears new is just a combination of older things."[4]

With Gulick's guidance, Naismith realized that a ball was a necessity since every popular team sport required one. Most sports that used a small ball required some sort of bat, stick, or racket to direct the

Dr. James Naismith invented the game of basketball in 1891.

THE YOUNG MEN'S CHRISTIAN ASSOCIATION

The Young Men's Christian Association (YMCA) was founded in 1844 by George Williams and a group of his associates in London, England, as a response to the unhealthy social conditions that existed in the large cities of the day. It attempted to substitute Bible study and prayer for life on the streets. The organization soon spread around the world, reaching North America in 1851. The first American branch was organized in Boston, Massachusetts. A century later, the number of local chapters approached two thousand.

The goal of the YMCA is to develop high standards of Christian character among children, teenagers, and adults. It attempts to do so through group activities and citizenship training. In addition to sports programs, these activities include camping, education, and public affairs projects. The organization assists troops in times of war, and was instrumental in helping to form the United Service Organization (USO), which, among other things, sends performers to entertain troops overseas.

Interestingly enough, basketball was not the only sport invented for use in YMCA classes. In 1895, William G. Morgan, director of the branch in Holyoke, Massachusetts, was looking for an activity his class of businessmen could play. He came up with a kind of team handball that used a net. His invention was called volleyball.

sphere. For simplicity's sake, Naismith therefore decided on a large ball. This could be caught and thrown by most people with little practice. A leather soccer ball was his ball of choice.

Sports such as football and rugby depended on carrying, or running with, a ball. To be stopped, the ballcarrier had to be tackled. Since Naismith's activity would be played indoors in a gymnasium, tackling would be too dangerous. His solution was to make passing the ball—or batting it with the hands—an essential element of play.

The final component of the game to be decided upon was scoring. Games that involved some sort of ground-level goal,

like hockey, soccer, and lacrosse, required the ball or puck to be shot, thrown, or kicked at the goal with great force. Again, this was not the ideal situation in a gymnasium setting. Naismith's thoughts drifted back to his childhood days in Canada. He later reminisced,

I recalled from my boyhood in the lumbering camps of Canada that when we played a game called "Duck on a Rock," a hurled ball might send the "duck" farther, but that a tossed ball was far more accurate. . . . Like "Duck on a Rock," the goal should be one that could not be rushed, and that the ball could not be slammed through. This called for a goal with a horizontal opening, high enough so the ball would have to be tossed into it, rather than being thrown.[5]

Scoring with such a goal would necessitate skill and have the added benefit of making it harder to block a player's shots and prevent scores.

The next morning, Naismith approached the school's superintendent of buildings—James "Pop" Stebbins—and asked for a pair of eighteen-inch square boxes to be used as goals. Stebbins did not have any, but suggested a replacement—two old round peach baskets. Naismith took the baskets and attached them to the lower rail of the balcony in the gym. As luck would have it, the height of the rail happened to be exactly ten feet. Like ninety feet between bases in baseball, this height has withstood the test of time and proven to be just the right height for the basket.

The Original Thirteen Rules

With the equipment decided upon, it was now time to write down the game's guidelines. Naismith did so and had the school's stenographer, Miss Lyons, type them up. He posted the game's original thirteen rules on the gym bulletin board for all to see. They read as follows:

Dr. Naismith's new game had to be played indoors and did not include the tackling prevalent in sports such as rugby (pictured).

The ball to be an ordinary Association football.

1. The ball may be thrown in any direction with one or both hands.
2. The ball may be batted in any direction with one or both hands (never with the fist).

 GEORGE GABLER

Although James Naismith is universally accepted as the inventor of basketball, there is another person who made a claim to being the game's originator. George Gabler was a physician and physical training instructor at a YMCA in Holyoke, Massachusetts. Shortly before his death in 1943, he related his version of the game's birth to Bill Keating, the sports editor of the *Holyoke Daily Transcript.*

According to Gabler's account, he invented the game with the help of two other YMCA instructors, one of whom—William Morgan—was the inventor of volleyball. The first game was played in either 1885 or 1890. Gabler claimed to have introduced the game to Naismith, who supposedly then stole the idea.

The notion that the religious Naismith—who would be ordained a Presbyterian minister in 1916—would steal credit for another's invention seems hard to believe, especially since the two men were friends. According to Keating, Gabler told him the story but requested that he not repeat it. "I don't want you to use this story until I have passed on," Gabler told Keating, according to Robert W. Peterson in *Cages to Jump Shots.* "I don't want to hurt my good friend . . . Naismith." Unfortunately, Gabler's claims are unverifiable, since a 1943 fire destroyed records at the Holyoke YMCA and Keating has since passed on.

3. A player cannot run with the ball. The player must throw it from the spot on which he catches it; allowance to be made for a man who catches the ball when running at a good speed.
4. The ball must be held in or between the hands; the arms or body must not be used for holding it.
5. No shouldering, holding, pushing, tripping, or striking, in any way the person of an opponent shall be allowed; the first infringement of this rule by any person shall count as a foul, the second shall disqualify him until the next goal is made, or, if there was evident intent to injure the person for the whole of the game, no substitute allowed.
6. A foul is striking at the ball with the fist, violation of Rules 3, 4, and such as described in Rule 5.
7. If either side makes three consecutive fouls, it shall count a goal for the opponents. (Consecutive means without the opponents in the meantime making a foul.)
8. A goal shall be made when the ball is thrown or batted from the grounds into the basket and stays there, providing those defending the goal do not touch or disturb the goal. If the ball rests on the edge and the opponent moves the basket, it shall count as a goal.
9. When the ball goes out of bounds, it shall be thrown into the field and

played by the person first touching it. In case of a dispute, the umpire shall throw it straight into the field. The thrower-in is allowed five seconds. If he holds it longer it shall go to the opponent. If any side persists in delaying the game, the umpire shall call a foul on them.

10. The umpire shall be the judge of the men and shall note the fouls and notify the referee when three consecutive fouls have been made. He shall have power to disqualify men according to Rule 5.

11. The referee shall be judge of the ball and shall decide when the ball is in play, in bounds, to which side it belongs, and shall keep the time. He shall decide when a goal has been made, and keep account of the goals, with any other duties that are usually performed by a referee.

12. The time shall be two fifteen minute halves, with five minutes rest between.

13. The side making the most goals in that time shall be declared the winners. In case of a draw, the game may, by agreement of the captains, be continued until another goal is made.[6]

When the students reported for class that early December day in 1891, Naismith selected two captains who divided the students into two nine-man teams. He tossed the ball up to begin play, adopting a move used in rugby. Unfamiliarity with the rules caused many players to spend a good bit of time in the penalty area, but the game was a rousing success. "It was the start of the first basketball game," said Naismith, "and the finish of the trouble with that class."[7] Although Naismith suggested years later that several scores were made that day, other accounts report that the contest ended in a score of 1–0.

Each day, the class started at 11:30 in the morning. By noontime, the game was under way. As the days went by, more and more spectators could be found in the gym taking in—and enjoying—the proceedings.

Within a couple of weeks, the men departed for their homes during Christmas break. They took the game with them, spreading the word to YMCAs all across the region. When the future secretaries returned to Springfield, one of them, Frank Mahan, suggested the game be called "Naismith ball." Naismith voted it down, however, and the simpler "basket ball" was decided upon instead. (The name became one word in 1920.) So was born the game of George Mikan, Wilt Chamberlain, and Michael Jordan.

"Basket Ball"

On January 15, 1892, the *Triangle* (the school's newspaper) carried the first written account of the new game, titled "Basket Ball." The article, written by Naismith, never mentioned the game's creator.

In the article, Naismith allowed that teams might consist of anywhere from three to forty players, but suggested nine per side as the ideal. Three offensive forwards, sometimes called "wings" or "attacks," would be stationed closest to the basket and be the team's best scorers. Three defenders or backs—two guards and a goalkeeper—would be positioned closest to the opposing team's basket. Between the two groups would be three players called "centers."

Nine of the students in Naismith's class of eighteen organized a team and played games throughout the region. The nine men on that first team were Lyman W. Archibald, William R. Chase, William H. Davis, Eugene S. Libby, Finlay G. MacDonald, Frank Mahan, T. Duncan Patton, Edwin P. Ruggles, and John G. Thompson. According to reports, the Springfield nine went undefeated in games played that winter and spring. As more and more people became exposed to the sport, basketball quickly became a favorite pastime at YMCAs across the country.

It was during this period that the first women's team was formed. According to Naismith, a group of female teachers from nearby Buckingham Grade School was observing one of the Springfield team's games. After being approached by one of the teachers, Naismith agreed to teach them his new sport. The teachers proceeded to form the first women's squad. A young

Dr. James Naismith (middle row, right) poses with the nine players who formed his first basketball team.

BASQUETTE

Women have enjoyed playing basketball almost as long as men. For more than half a century, women played a variation of the game known as *basquette*. Interestingly enough, the game came about primarily because of a mistake.

Soon after James Naismith introduced his new sport, he was besieged by a torrent of letters from people all over the country requesting the rules for his invention. One such request came from Clara Baer, a physical education instructor at Newcomb College in New Orleans, Louisiana. Naismith responded with a set of printed instructions that included a diagram of the playing area. On the diagram were lines indicating the areas where Naismith thought the players could best be positioned. Unfortunately, Baer misread the sketch. She thought the lines indicated zones in which the players were meant to stay. She eventually wrote a rule book for women, renaming the game *basquette.*

Naismith never bothered correcting her mistake, since he was only interested in seeing his invention used as a physical recreation, not as a competitive sport. The game took the form of a six-on-six contest, with players required to remain in their half of the court at all times. This seemed logical, since the men's game was thought to be too strenuous for women. It was not until the 1960s that the rules were again modified, bringing the sport into line with the men's version.

woman named Maude E. Sherman was one of the players on that team. Sherman would marry Naismith in 1894.

The Later Years

Naismith remained at Springfield until 1895. He then left New England to continue his studies at Gross Medical College in Denver, Colorado. He took a job as the physical education director of the Denver YMCA to help pay for his courses. After getting his medical degree in 1898, Naismith left Denver and moved on to the University of Kansas in Lawrence, where he remained for the next thirty-nine years. Naismith was first a chapel director, then a professor of physical education at the school. In time, he introduced basketball and became the school's first basketball coach. He did not believe in coaching as we know it today, however. When his friend—and eventual successor—Forrest "Phog" Allen told him he was going to coach a college team, Naismith replied, "Why Forrest, basketball is just a game to play. You don't coach it."[8]

Naismith always downplayed the competitive aspects of the game he invented. He had little interest in winning contests, being more concerned with the physical benefits to the players. After twelve years as coach, he stepped down with a career coaching mark of 55 wins and 60 losses. Ironically, he is the only coach in Kansas's long basketball history to log a losing record.

AMOS ALONZO STAGG

Amos Alonzo Stagg's name is generally associated with the sport of football. As an offensive right end at Yale University in 1889, he was named to the first All-America football team ever chosen. Also a star baseball player in college, he passed up a chance to play professional baseball and turned to football coaching. He was a football head coach for a remarkable fifty-seven years, winning a total of 314 games. He was responsible for so many innovations that legendary Notre Dame coach Knute Rockne (quoted in Dave Anderson's *The Story of Football*) once said, "All football comes from Stagg."

Following his graduation from Yale, he attended Springfield College. He was a teammate of James Naismith, who later introduced Stagg to basketball. When Stagg left to coach at Chicago University, he took Naismith's invention along with him and became the college's coach. It was his Chicago University squad that traveled to Iowa City, where they beat a YMCA team representing the University of Iowa in the first five-on-a-side college game on record, on January 16, 1896.

In addition to coaching football at Chicago for forty years, Stagg also coached seven Western Conference basketball championship teams. From 1917 to 1930, he conducted the National High

Amos Alonzo Stagg coached seven Western Conference basketball champion teams.

School Tournament, which helped standardize play. His contributions to the game of basketball were so great that in 1959 he was one of eight contributors—along with Naismith, Phog Allen, Luther Gulick, Ed Hickox, Ralph Moran, Harold Olsen, and Oswald Tower—elected to the Basketball Hall of Fame on the first ballot ever.

In 1936, Naismith traveled to the summer Olympics in Berlin, Germany, to see basketball played as an Olympic sport for the first time. (It had been a "demonstration" sport in the 1904 Games in St. Louis.) Just three years later, the first National Collegiate Athletic Association (NCAA) basketball tournament was held, in response to the maiden National Invitation Tournament that had successfully debuted in March 1938. Naismith could never have imagined the impact his game would have on future generations. He passed away on November 28, 1939, shortly after his seventy-eighth birthday.

CHAPTER 2

The Evolution of a Simple Game

IN THE HUNDRED-plus years since its invention, the game of basketball has probably changed more than baseball or football over similar time periods. Of the thirteen rules that governed the first contest back in 1891, perhaps half a dozen are still in effect in something akin to their original form.

Naismith's vision of a noncontact activity that could be enjoyed by all simply for fun seemed unrealistic right from the start. Since the number of players involved in any particular game might total as many as forty per side, it was practically impossible for a referee to notice all infractions. Games often deteriorated into little more than wrestling matches, with players mobbing the unfortunate who happened to end up holding the ball. Early competitions might end with no more than a single basket or two being scored. It would be some time before the game evolved into the one played by millions of people around the world today.

Basketball's Ruling Bodies

James Naismith was obviously the authority on basketball in the game's formative years. When he left Springfield in the summer of 1895, Luther Halsey Gulick, the chairman of the physical education department, took over the responsibility of editing the rules. Eventually, Gulick formed the first basketball rules committee—called the Basketball Co-Operating Committee—to oversee the sport. As the pastime spread, however, the YMCA asked the Amateur

Athletic Union (AAU) to assume this responsibility.

In time, as with other sports, money would become an issue in basketball. Players eventually were paid to perform, thus becoming professionals. The professional teams soon broke away from the AAU and formed their own leagues. The *Reach Official Basketball Guide,* published in 1901, became the source used by professionals for the next quarter of a century. By that time, colleges had adopted their own rule book—the *Official Collegiate Basketball Guide,* published by the Spalding Company in 1905. The NCAA took over publication of the college rules in 1908. The different rule books resulted in variations in the style of play over the early years of the twentieth century.

Dr. Luther Gulick succeeded Naismith as editor of the rules of basketball.

Changes in Equipment

Naismith recommended nine players per side as the ideal number for his game, and most early contests followed this proposal. By 1893, YMCA standards decreed that the number be based on the size of the playing surface: for gymnasiums of eighteen hundred square feet or less, five men per side; from eighteen hundred to three thousand square feet, seven men per side; and for more than three thousand square feet, nine men per side. Four years later, the number of players was fixed at the current five per side.

By that time, several other significant changes had already gone into effect. Peach baskets had been replaced by fifteen-inch cylindrical wire baskets that were introduced by Lew Allen. The height of the goal remained at ten feet. However, rather than having someone climb up and remove the ball from the enclosure when a score was made, a pole was used to punch the ball free. By the mid-1890s, the Narragansett Machine Company of Providence, Rhode Island, introduced an eighteen-inch iron hoop from which hung braided cord netting. After a basket was scored, the referee pulled on a hanging cord that was attached to the net. This cord lifted the net and released the ball.

The ball, too, saw refinements. The first official basketball was larger than a soccer ball, and slightly bigger than the ball in use today. It was produced by the Overman Wheel Company in Chicopee Falls, Massachusetts, and consisted of four panels of tanned cowhide, stuffed with a rubber bladder and held together with laces similar to a football. The laces were thick enough to cause erratic bounces if the ball hit the rim at just the right angle.

Another change in equipment was the introduction of the backboard in 1895. Despite what may seem obvious, the backboard was not introduced to aid the players in shooting. Instead, its purpose was to prevent spectators from interfering with play. Fans sitting behind the baskets could reach over the rail and guide their team's shots toward the goal, or knock opponents' shots away. A four-foot-by-six-foot wire or wood screen was inserted behind the hoop to eliminate this problem. Wood interfered with the spectators' view, so wire screen became the backboard of choice.

The wire variety, however, presented its own problems. After re-

peated shots, the screen became dented. The home team, being more familiar with the board's quirks, had a decided advantage. The problems associated with wire and wood were eliminated when plate-glass backboards were introduced in 1909.

The appearance of the players on the court was also decidedly different from today. There was no official uniform at the beginning, so players wore the clothes they normally wore to physical education class. This might range from trousers and short-sleeved shirts to football pads to track shorts. The Spalding Company advertised a basketball outfit in its 1901 catalog. Suggested were knee-length pants and either a

Early basketball players shoot at a peach-basket hoop.

FREE THROWS

No one understands the importance of free throws more than former Boston Celtics superstar Larry Bird. "Free throws," Bird states in an April 13, 1998, *Sports Illustrated* article, "are the key to *all* games."

Theoretically, the shot should be one of the easiest in basketball. The player stands at a line just fifteen feet from the basket. He has ten seconds in which to shoot the ball, with no one guarding him and no arms being waved in his face. Surprisingly, many modern-day players seem to have more problems with this relatively simple action than players of the past.

The surest method for shooting free throws has proven to be a two-handed, underhand motion. Rick Barry, the best free throw shooter in the history of the National Basketball Association, used this technique to make 90 percent of his shots over a fourteen-year period. Unfortunately, the movements involved do not look macho enough for modern players. Wilt Chamberlain, known for his struggles at the line, tried the method for a while with some success. However, he soon gave it up. *Sports Illustrated*'s Michael Bamberger quotes Chamberlain: "I felt silly," Chamberlain wrote in his autobiography, "like a sissy."

The fact that many of the greatest athletes in the world cannot make the shot even seven times out of ten suggests that the mental approach is also important. Perhaps this is why the record for the most consecutive free throws converted is held by a former dairy farmer. Over a period of three days in 1977, Ted St. Martin made 2,036 consecutive free throws during an appearance at a shopping mall in Jacksonville, Florida. The NBA record, held by Michael Williams of the Minnesota Timberwolves, is 97.

Celtics great Larry Bird was one of the most precise free throw shooters.

sleeveless or quarter-length-sleeve shirt. Two years later, Spalding advertised the first suction sole basketball shoes, guaranteed to give better traction. The basic construction of these canvas high-tops remained the same for more than half a century.

With better equipment, the talents of the players shone through even more. The smarter ones were always on the lookout for ways to use the rules to their advantage. New guidelines were adopted in an effort to close these "loopholes," and make the game even more enjoyable for players and spectators alike.

Rule Changes

In Naismith's original guidelines, each goal counted for a single point. There were no foul shots, with players temporarily removed from the game for committing infractions. When free throws were introduced, they were taken from a distance of twenty feet. This was reduced to the current fifteen feet in 1895. The number of points awarded for any basket was briefly increased to three before being reduced in 1896 to two for a field goal and one for a free throw. The rules remained without change until the three-point shot came into existence in the 1980s.

The center jump, or jump ball, played a much more important role in the game than it does today. The referee, who stood at the sidelines, would toss the ball up between the two opposing centers, who stood at midcourt, to begin each half of play. The players would try to tip the ball to their teammates or possibly catch it themselves.

The ball was also put into play this way after any score. Not only did this slow down the pace of the game, it also gave a decided advantage to a team whose center could consistently control the tipoff that put the ball in play. The procedure would be followed for most of basketball's first half century. In 1937, the center jump was eliminated after successful free throws, and after successful field goals the following year. Naismith disagreed with the ruling. "To award the ball to a team after a goal is scored," he wrote, "takes away much of the thrill that is present in an opening play. A crowd does not rise to its feet in excitement at the start of a play when the ball is simply given to a team."[9] Most people disagreed with him, however, and with play now sped up, interest in the game became greater.

By 1982, the jump ball had been eliminated even further. It is now employed only

The jump ball is now only employed at the beginning of a game and at the start of overtime.

at the beginning of the game, and to start overtime periods. On other occasions when a jump ball is called for, teams are given possession on an alternating basis.

Dribbling

The concept of dribbling the ball in order to advance it was not thought up by Naismith. It developed, as sometimes happens, as a method of getting around the rules of the day. In order to get away from an opposing player, the player with the ball would roll it a short distance away, then run to catch it again before his opponent could reach it. Technically, he did not have possession when the ball was bouncing free. The more resourceful players soon realized they could control the ball by bouncing it and catching it, over and over. Advancing the ball with this style of play became known as the dribble game, and Yale University was one of its early practitioners.

Some of the more creative players recognized that the same rule would apply if they hit the ball into the air rather than on the ground. They would race down the court continually tapping the ball a couple of inches above their hands. To prevent this maneuver, a new rule required that any tapping of the ball take place above the player's head.

Guidelines dealing with dribbling evolved around the turn of the twentieth century. In 1898, it was decreed that players could not touch the ball with both hands more than once while dribbling. As Luther Gulick wrote, "The object of the rule is to largely do away with dribbling. . . . Dribbling has introduced all of the objectionable features that are hurting the game. It gives the advantage to heavy men and to rough play."[10]

A player could, however, bounce the ball with one hand as often as he wanted, even if he stopped moving between bounces. (Today this action, known as a double dribble, is no longer allowed.) The next year saw it accepted that a player could alternate hands while dribbling.

A 1901 rule made it illegal for a player to take a shot, or score points, after dribbling the ball. The player had to pass the ball to a teammate before taking a shot at the basket. This standard remained in effect until 1915, when the ball handler was again allowed to shoot.

Miscellaneous Rules

Naismith's ninth rule stated that when a ball went out-of-bounds, it was to be put back into play by the first team touching it. The result was a series of mad scrambles whenever the ball left the court. This caused players, officials, and spectators alike to be put in danger of bodily harm. In 1914, the rule was changed so that an opponent of the player who caused the ball to go out of play was allowed to put it back in.

The 1930s saw a series of rules put into effect with the purpose of keeping the action on the court moving. One of the most

REFEREES

Refereeing a basketball game is one of the toughest jobs in sports. Due to the fast pace of the game and the constant movement of the players, it is impossible for a person to see every violation that might occur. Such has been the case since the game was first played.

Naismith's original rules prohibited shouldering, holding, pushing, tripping, or striking an opponent in any way. These violations were impossible to prevent, however. An account of an early game quoted in Robert W. Peterson's *Cages to Jump Shots* reported that "there were twenty or more fairly good wrestling matches going on simultaneously, and occasional scientific sparring exhibitions took place without in any slightest way interfering with the progress of the game." Punching or tripping might be detected without too much trouble, but shouldering, holding, and pushing was another matter altogether.

In addition to failing to see or call violations, referees were also intimidated by the crowd, which often called for their blood if decisions went against the home team. Some officials solved this problem by constantly favoring the home club, resulting in complaints from opposing teams. No one, it seemed, could make everyone happy.

Rule changes added to the difficulty of the job. Not only did referees have to watch the players for physical contact, they also had to be on the lookout for half-court violations, three-second infractions, goaltending, traveling, zone defenses, and so on.

With such a prodigious task facing them, it is only fair that the best officials be given credit for performing so well. The game could not have become successful without the efforts of men like Pat Kennedy, Jim Enright, John Nucatola, and Earl Strom, just four of the referees inducted into the Naismith Memorial Basketball Hall of Fame.

---

important of these was the ten-second backcourt violation, enacted in 1933, which required the offensive team—the one with the ball—to move it past the midcourt line within ten seconds. This prevented teams from stalling on offense. Three years later, it became a violation for an offensive player to remain within the foul lanes for more than three seconds at a time.

Other rules refined over the years have concerned goaltending, or blocking shots on their downward flight to the basket. Defensive goaltending was outlawed in 1944, and offensive goaltending, fourteen years

later. A further attempt to limit the effectiveness of the big man (specifically, Lew Alcindor, later known as Kareem Abdul-Jabbar) was tried by the college game in 1968 when the dunk shot was prohibited. The ban did not last long, however, with the shot being made legal again in 1977.

With each new rule change, the delicate balance between offense and defense has become more finely tuned. The game has become faster and more fun to watch. When money entered the picture, the best players were given even more incentive to perfect their skills.

CHAPTER 3

The Pros Come of Age

MOST GAMES PLAYED during basketball's early years were between YMCA teams. One of the foremost clubs of the era was the Trenton Basketball Team, representing the Trenton, New Jersey, YMCA. By 1896, the team claimed to be the national champion, having soundly defeated most of its opponents. That fall, however, problems developed with the YMCA. Many YMCA leaders had become upset with the roughness of the game and the way in which it dominated gym time. As an 1894 YMCA publication commented, "The game could never and should never be allowed to take the place of all other exercise in the gymnasium."[11] For whatever reason, the Trenton team was forced to move its home games to the local Masonic Temple.

The First Professionals

Trenton's first game in 1896 was played on November 7 against the Brooklyn YMCA. An admission charge of twenty-five cents per seat (fifteen cents for standing room) was collected at the door. Led by team captain Fred Cooper and Albert Bratton (the two men credited with popularizing the short passing game in which a series of quick passes were used to move the ball), Trenton defeated Brooklyn by a score of 16–1. For their participation in the event, each Trenton player reportedly received fifteen dollars (although five dollars was a more likely amount). The game is generally considered to signify the beginning of professional basketball in the United States. From that point on, team members generally received a portion of the ticket sales.

The Trenton-Brooklyn match was noteworthy for another reason. According to the rules of the day, when a ball went out-of-bounds, the first player to touch it gained possession. This resulted in mad scrambles, and occasional injuries to those sitting in the stands. With spectators now required to pay for their seats, it was not good policy to leave them open to these dangers.

In order to prevent such melees, Trenton's team manager, Fred Padderatz, came up with the idea of enclosing the court with a twelve-foot-high wire mesh fence. One legend has it that he was inspired by a local sportswriter who wrote that "these fellows play like monkeys and should be put in a cage."[12]

In addition to keeping the paying fans safe, this innovation sped up the game, since out-of-bounds play was eliminated. Referee Marvin A. Riley related that the cage "did make the game faster and more enjoyable for the spectators."[13] Two years later, the first professional circuit—the National Basketball League—required cages for all of its games. Eventually, many courts in the East had such cages, although the innovation was rarely found farther west. Basketball players soon came to be called "cagers." In time, rope netting replaced the wire mesh, much to the relief of the participants. As early star Barney Sedran explained, "Players would be thrown against the wire and most of us would get cut. The court was covered with blood."[14]

By 1888, the AAU had been established to regulate amateur sports. Nine years later, it sponsored the first national basketball championship tournament in New York

Cages made of rope netting replaced the wire mesh cages introduced in the late nineteenth century to prevent injuries to fans.

City. A team representing the Twenty-third Street YMCA won the title. Soon after, the club announced it was turning professional. The team was banned from using the YMCA gym and forced to take to the road. The New York Wanderers thus became the first of the famous barnstorming basketball teams—clubs that traveled from place to place to play their games rather than having a "home" court.

The Wanderers played games throughout the East, extending as far north as New England. In Lowell, Massachusetts, Hood's Laboratories asked the players to endorse one of the company's products. By receiving five dollars per man (plus a free bottle of the company's tonic), the Wanderers set the stage for the Michael Jordans of the present day by becoming the first basketball players to earn money from endorsements.

The First Professional Leagues

In 1898, the first professional league was born. It called itself the National Basketball League (NBL), and consisted of six teams—the Trenton, New Jersey, Nationals; the Millville, New Jersey Glassblowers; the Camden, New Jersey, Electrics; the Philadelphia Clover Wheelmen; the Germantown, Pennsylvania, Nationals; and the Hancock Athletic Association of Philadelphia. Trenton defeated Millville that year to take the first championship. Players earned a minimum of $3.75 a week in the league,

which lasted five more years. It eventually was forced to disband when other leagues began luring away its star players.

No fewer than a dozen circuits came into existence in the first two decades of the twentieth century, all in the northeastern United States. These new associations—the two most prominent of which were the Central League (1906–1912) and the Eastern League (1909–1923)—flared briefly on the pro basketball scene, then faded into obscurity just as quickly. Players sometimes performed for more than one team at the same time. There were no yearly contracts, and players would offer their services to clubs on a game-by-game basis, going with the team that made the best offer. Of those early days, player Joe Lapchick recalled, "My earnings increased by leaps and bounds. I played one manager against the other and sometimes got as much as $75 a game. I bargained with the managers for every game." [15]

This lack of stability was a major factor leading to the demise of these early operations. Another was the size of the towns where they played. With the majority of clubs located in smaller cities (such as Chester, Pennsylvania; Haverhill, Massachusetts; and East Liverpool, Ohio), it was rare for a game to receive national attention. Individual leagues were done in by a variety of other factors, such as the excessive length of team schedules, the raucous behavior on the part of players, and the onset of World

ED WACHTER

One of the first stars of pro basketball's early days was Ed Wachter. The six-foot-one-inch center dominated the game for the first two decades of the twentieth century, mostly with the Troy, New York, Trojans.

Wachter began playing professionally in 1903 with the Ware team of the Western Massachusetts League. When Ware sent him to the Haverhill club of the New England League in exchange for one hundred dollars, it marked the first case of a basketball player being sold.

Wachter's Troy team dominated both the Hudson River and New York State Leagues. The team pioneered many innovations, including the fast break and the bounce pass. Years later, Wachter proudly recalled the words of James Naismith after basketball's inventor had seen a game in which Wachter performed. As quoted in *Cages to Jump Shots*, Naismith said, "You boys play the game of basketball as it was intended to be played, by passing the ball from one player to another until a player reaches an advantageous position to make a try for the basket."

In 1912, with Wachter's encouragement, the New York State League adopted the practice of having the player who was fouled shoot his own free throws. Prior to this, one designated player on each team did all the free throw shooting.

When his playing days were over, Wachter coached college basketball at Albany State and Rensselaer, both in New York, and at Williams and Harvard, both in Massachusetts. This was all the more impressive since Wachter himself never even attended high school.

War I. Since many teams played their games in local armories, the facilities were no longer available for use with more pressing matters at hand.

Players were not the only ones who jumped leagues. Occasionally entire teams did so. By 1920, the problem had reached such proportions that the four leagues in existence at the time—the Eastern League, the Interstate League, the New York State League, and the Pennsylvania League—decided to do something about it. A three-man National Commission was set up in an attempt to bring stability to the world of professional basketball. Among other things, the resulting National Agreement forbade

players from participating in more than one league and set up a tournament to decide a "world champion." Unfortunately, the grand plan was ineffective. The Interstate League soon backed out, and player jumping continued.

The Barnstormers

While the professional leagues often struggled, other teams eked out an existence by barnstorming around the country. One of the most famous and successful of those early clubs was the Buffalo Germans. The Germans began in 1895 as a team of fourteen-year-olds led by Allie Heerdt and Ed Miller. In 1901, the club made headlines by winning

The Buffalo Germans dominated the opposition in the early twentieth century, winning 111 games in a row during one stretch.

the basketball tournament held at the Pan-American Exposition in Buffalo. Three years later, it took part in the tournament held as part of the 1904 Olympic Games. Again the Germans came out on top, winning all five of their games. (They did not win gold medals, since basketball was only a demonstration sport and not an official competition.) Now claiming the title of "world champions," the Germans turned professional following the Olympiad.

Over the course of twenty-nine years, the Germans compiled an enviable record. Their mark of 761 wins and 85 defeats included an amazing string of 111 victories in a row. Most of their games were against college and YMCA teams. Buffalo was a good distance away from the nearest professional league, so the Germans rarely played pro clubs. They eventually joined the new American Basketball League in 1925, calling themselves the Buffalo Bisons. After one unsuccessful season, the team disbanded. In 1961, the Buffalo Germans became the third team enshrined in the Basketball Hall of Fame as a complete unit.

The club that ended the Germans' remarkable streak was Frank J. Basloe's 31st Separate Company of Herkimer, New York. Basloe was a native of Hungary who did much to spread basketball's popularity in the Midwest. He organized his first professional team in 1903, when he was just sixteen years of age. Over the next twenty years, his clubs won 1,324 games while losing 127. In doing so, his teams traveled nearly one hundred thousand miles. After defeating the Germans, Basloe promoted his team (also known at various times as the Oswego Indians and Basloe's Globe Trotters) as world champions.

While his squad entertained fans throughout the Midwest, Basloe used his wiles to bring money into the club's coffers. A promoter at heart, he would secretly incite fans in the stands into throwing things at his team on the court. He then negotiated for more money in order to allow his men to continue playing under such dangerous circumstances. Another favorite ploy was to surrender the team's "official" world championship banner to any club that defeated them. Of course there was a charge for the prize, usually averaging around fifty dollars. Unbeknownst to the other manager, Basloe kept a supply of the five-dollar banners in the trunk of his car.

The Early College Game

Although basketball was centered around the YMCA in the beginning, it soon spread to college campuses. The first school squads played games against teams from local YMCAs. The first informal game between two colleges took place on February

---

THE PASSAIC HIGH SCHOOL "WONDER TEAMS"

The professional basketball record for consecutive wins is 33, set by the Los Angeles Lakers in the 1971–1972 season. John Wooden's University of California at Los Angeles clubs won 88 games in a row from 1971 to 1974 to set the college standard. Coach Ernest Blood's Passaic (New Jersey) High School "Wonder Teams," however, have them both beat.

From 1915 to 1924, Blood's Passaic compiled an incredible record of 200 victories against a single loss. Their only defeat came at the hands of Union Hill in the finals of New Jersey's first state tournament in 1919. After that, his squad won 147 games in a row. After he gave up the coaching position, the school won an additional 12 games to give it a grand total of 159 consecutive victories. The streak was finally ended on February 6, 1925, when Passaic was defeated by Hackensack.

Blood's coaching philosophy included running a wide-open, fast-paced offense. By following a total conditioning program, his boys were in better shape than their opponents and were able to run them into the ground. Twelve times his team outscored the opposition by 100 or more points. During the 1921–1922 season, his squad averaged nearly 70 points a game, or twice what the average team scored.

9, 1895. In a nine-on-nine contest, the Minnesota State School of Agriculture defeated Hamline by a count of 9–3. The first game between five-man squads matched the University of Chicago against the University of Iowa on January 16, 1896. The Iowa team, however, was actually a YMCA club made up of university students. What is generally recognized as the first five-man intercollegiate game did not take place until more than a year later. This occurred on March 20, 1897, when Yale University bested the University of Pennsylvania, 32–10. College conferences soon were formed, with the Intercollegiate League, the New England League, the Western Conference, and the Southern Intercollegiate Athletic Association being among the first.

The first college basketball championship was held as part of the 1904 Olympics, following the open competition that was won by the Buffalo Germans. Ohio's Hiram College, Massachusetts' Wheaton College, and Utah's Latter Day Saints University (now known as Brigham Young University) competed in the tournament, with Hiram emerging victorious. More and more schools began to schedule games outside of their local regions. These trips were instrumental in spreading basketball to new parts of the country.

The college game differed from the one played in YMCAs in several ways. Dribbling, which required more skill and stamina, played a larger part in the college game, where players were generally younger

This building in Springfield, Massachusetts, was home to an early YMCA, an organization around which basketball was centered before it spread to college campuses.

and in better shape. Coaching also developed on the collegiate level. New strategies were refined, including the passing game and the zone defense. The foremost coach of the era was Joseph Raycroft, whose University of Chicago teams, led by four-time All-American center John Schommer, dominated their opponents. One of the highlights of pre–World War I intercollegiate play was Chicago's victory over Pennsylvania for the 1908 national title. The game was won on Schommer's last-second, eighty-foot desperation heave, which somehow found the mark. Other college stars of the era included high-scoring Christian Steinmetz of the University of Wisconsin and Pat Page of the University of Chicago, often called the greatest all-around player of the day.

The Original Celtics

The end of World War I found interest in sports explode all across the United States. Fans avidly read newspapers to follow the exploits of their heroes in what has been called the "Golden Age of Sports." Professional basketball, however, lagged behind baseball and football. Many operations folded, and the start of the 1923–1924 season found only the Metropolitan Basketball League still operative.

Amateur teams, on the other hand, continued to flourish. Fans ardently followed the accomplishments of their local college teams. Coaching was more sophisticated at the college level, and teams were always

making adjustments to new offensive and defensive schemes. The result was a crisper style of play that fans found more appealing.

The pros still played in wire or mesh cages. With the area of play restricted, it was no surprise that the increased amount of contact inspired a rougher, more uneven style of play. Fights were not uncommon, and games were often won by the more intimidating team. As former player Rody Cooney explained, "It wasn't a matter of speed and brains. It was more a case of brute force, hard tactics, and all the dirty tricks you could put into it without arousing the antagonisms of the officials or spectators."[16]

The most dominant professional team of the 1920s was the Original Celtics. It came into existence in 1914, beginning as a teenage settlement-house team. As semipros, the club was known as the New York Celtics before briefly disbanding. When team owner James Furey re-formed the team in 1918, he changed its name to the Original Celtics.

Sparked by such stars as sharpshooting Johnny Beckman, pivotman Swede Grimstead, and skillful ball handler Dutch Dehnert, the team quickly gained a reputation as one of New York's best. Former New York Whirlwinds' stars Nat Holman and Chris Leonard were soon added, further strengthening an already impressive squad. Six-foot-five-inch Joe Lapchick joined in 1923, becoming the team's anchor at center. With his great leaping ability, Lapchick was almost certain to control the center jumps

ORIGINAL CELTICS

Johnny Beckman

Dutch Dehnert

Joe Lapchick

Nat Holman

The Original Celtics played strategic basketball, which included switching on defense, and the use of the pivot play on offense.

after each basket. In this way, the team maintained control of the ball for the greater portion of its contests.

The Celtics played most of their home games in New York's Madison Square Garden. Their greatest success, however, came as a barnstorming squad. They toured throughout the Northeast, Midwest, and South, winning legions of fans wherever they played.

Although other teams may have done so previously, the Celtics are usually credited with originating the idea of switching on de-

fense, and using the pivot play on offense. The latter, according to most accounts, was first used in the 1925–1926 season during a game against the Chattanooga Rail-Lites on one of the team's southern tours. Chattanooga employed what was known as a "standing guard." This player spent the entire game near the center of the opposition's foul lane, his sole purpose being to prevent easy drives to the basket. Dehnert counteracted this strategy by taking a position directly in front of the guard, with his back toward him. In this way, he was able to block the player's vision. Dehnert would get the ball and quickly throw a return pass to his teammate, who was cutting to the basket. If the defensive player attempted to get the ball by reaching around Dehnert, Dehnert would simply pivot, or swivel, in the opposite direction and score an easy goal. The play became so successful that handbills advertising the Celtics would urge fans to "See The Original Pivot Play Starring The One and Only 'Dutch' Dehnert!"[17]

Innovations such as the pivot play guaranteed the Celtics large crowds wherever they appeared. Furey assured team stability by paying his players good salaries. By remaining together, the players developed a cohesiveness that made them almost unbeatable. "They were magnificent ballhandlers," remembered Lapchick, "who played completely as a unit. The individual star was unknown, in fact, not even considered."[18] The Celtics are generally recognized as the greatest team of basketball's first half century.

The Renaissance

By the 1920s, the Harlem neighborhood in New York City had become the most famous black community in the country. Black artists from a variety of fields converged there, signaling the beginning of an unparalleled era of cultural diversity that came to be called the Harlem Renaissance.

In 1923, Robert J. Douglas, an enthusiastic supporter of organized sports for New York City African Americans, decided to form a professional basketball team. Looking for a place to play, he approached the owners of Harlem's Renaissance Casino,

The Renaissance overmatched opponents by playing a clean and exciting style of basketball.

The Harlem Globetrotters, an all black team founded by Abe Saperstein in 1927, became famous for its entertaining brand of basketball.

which had a large ballroom on its second floor. In exchange for use of the facility for games, Douglas offered to name the team the Renaissance.

The Rens, as the team was also called, played a clean, fast, exciting brand of basketball, featuring crisp passing and tight defense. Renaissance players did not use the roughhouse tactics employed by many other teams. As Hall of Famer Honey Russell recalled, "They just played basketball that was so good they didn't have to resort to any of the rough stuff." [19]

The Rens barnstormed throughout the region, taking on all comers, and were an immediate success. They were instrumental in popularizing the sport among black high

school and college students wherever they went. In time, only the Original Celtics could compete with the Rens as a gate attraction.

The golden age of the Rens was the 1930s, when the team featured stars such as Fats Jenkins, Pappy Ricks, Bruiser Saitch, Tarzan Cooper, and Wee Willie Smith. Toward the end of the decade, guard Pop Gates became the team's leading player.

The Rens' decade of dominance was highlighted in 1939 by their performance in the first World Tournament, sponsored by the Chicago *Herald-American.* The tournament was recognized by most pro players as the first real "world series" of basketball. The Rens won all four of their games, defeating Wisconsin's Oshkosh All-Stars, champions of the NBL, in the finals. Hall of Fame player and coach John Wooden called that Rens club "the greatest team I ever saw."[20] By the time the club disbanded a decade later, it had compiled a record of 2,318 wins and 381 losses over its twenty-six-year existence.

The Harlem Globetrotters

The Harlem Globetrotters came into existence as a barnstorming team in 1927. Called Saperstein's New York at the time (later, simply New York, then Saperstein's Harlem New York, and finally, Saperstein's Harlem Globetrotters), the team established a reputation with the help of the promotional skills of its founder, Abe Saperstein. The all-black Globetrotters, or Globies, played straight basketball for the first decade of their existence, and developed into one of the top teams of the era.

The Globies barnstormed throughout the country, often rolling over the much inferior competition. In part to ease the boredom of their one-sided victories, players began to develop show routines to entertain the fans and show off their skills. By the 1940s, their performances included much of the ball-handling magic and many of the comedy skits they are known for today.

They could still play "straight" basketball, however. In 1940, the Globies won the Chicago World Tournament by defeating the Chicago Bruins of the NBL in the final game. By the end of the decade, their enter-taining and playing skills had established them as the number one attraction on the basketball scene.

While barnstorming teams entertained fans across the country, the professional

EDDIE GOTTLIEB

No one was more involved in professional basketball, in more capacities, than Eddie Gottlieb. He helped organize the Philadelphia Sphas, a predominantly Jewish team that took its name from the South Philadelphia Hebrew Association. The Sphas, one of the top barnstorming teams of the 1920s, went on to dominate the American Basketball League and eventually won eleven titles. Gottlieb was also a business adviser to Abe Saperstein's Harlem Globetrotters and helped Saperstein promote Negro League baseball.

In 1946, the Basketball Association of America was formed. Gottlieb entered the Philadelphia Warriors as one of the league's charter members, and coached the team to the circuit's first championship. He became a driving force in the league and helped bring about the merger with the rival National Basketball League. As one of the National Basketball Association's (NBA) founding fathers, he held an important position as a member of the league's rules committee. His promotions helped gain exposure for the league and helped expand its fan base.

In his later years, Gottlieb spent his summers putting together the NBA schedule for the following season. For his service to the league, he was given a singular honor. The trophy given annually to the league's top rookie is known as the Eddie Gottlieb Award.

game remained a largely local phenomenon. College ball, on the other hand, was increasing in popularity.

Ned Irish and the College Boom

On January 19, 1931, a college basketball triple-header was staged at New York's Madison Square Garden. This was during the Great Depression, when millions of people were out of work. More than fourteen thousand spectators attended the games that were staged to raise money for Mayor Jimmy Walker's Committee for the Relief of the Unemployed and Needy. One of those who took note of the sport's exploding popularity was a sportswriter for the *New York World Telegram* named Ned Irish.

In 1933, Irish was assigned by his paper to cover a game at Manhattan College's gym. According to legend, because of the size of the crowd and the tightness of the gym, the only way the young reporter could gain entry was by crawling in through a window. In doing so, he tore a hole in his pants. The entire incident convinced Irish of the sport's burgeoning popularity. Basketball was ripe for a promotional blitz, and he was just the person to carry it through.

Irish quit his job with the newspaper and signed a contract to pro-

mote college basketball at Madison Square Garden. His first promotion was a double-header featuring teams from New York University, Indiana's Notre Dame, New York's St. John's, and Pennsylvania's Westminster. Held on December 29, 1934, the games attracted a crowd of more than sixteen thousand to the spacious arena. Irish followed up with seven other doubleheaders that 1934–1935 season, attracting a total of nearly one hundred thousand fans in all. The venture's overwhelming success as-

College basketball promoter Ned Irish.

sured New York of its standing as the center of the college basketball universe.

In future years, at Irish's behest, the top college teams from around the nation visited the Garden. One of the most prominent was from Stanford University in California.

Stanford's game against Long Island University (LIU) on December 30, 1936, proved to be especially significant. Coach Clair Bee's LIU team, the Blackbirds, had won 43 games in a row coming into the contest, and was a heavy favorite to continue its winning ways. The underdogs from Stanford, however, surprised the Blackbirds, upsetting them by a score of 45–31. The player who stole the show, and won over the hometown crowd, was a six-foot-three-inch junior named Hank Luisetti.

Luisetti scored 15 points that night to lead Stanford to victory. It was the way he shot, however, that garnered all the attention. Instead of planting himself firmly and shooting with two hands, as was the style of the day, Luisetti tossed the ball up with one hand, while lifting up slightly from the floor. The style of shooting horrified veterans like City College of New York coach—and former Original Celtic—Nat Holman. "If my boys ever shot one-handed," he grumbled, "I'd quit coaching."[21] Others, however, appreciated the shot's benefits. "It's merely a matter of efficiency," explained Luisetti. "I don't have to take time to get set when I shoot one-handed. That saves a half second. I can shoot while in

motion, and what probably is most important of all, I can shoot with accuracy."[22]

The LIU game gave Luisetti national attention. His pioneering style ushered in a new era, literally single-handedly. "We really didn't know what we were starting that night at Madison Square Garden," he later said. "We had no idea that we would bring on a revolution. And I had no notion of what that one game would mean to me."[23]

Within a short time, college players across the nation were experimenting with the new one-handed shot. Luisetti's effect on the game cannot be underestimated. He is remembered as one of the most influential figures in basketball's first half century.

The NIT and the NCAA Tournament

In 1938, with the center jump after each basket having been eliminated, college basketball's appeal as a spectator sport had been proven. The New York Metropolitan Basketball Writers sponsored the first National Invitation Tournament (NIT) at New York's Madison Square Garden. Six top teams from around the country—Bradley University in Peoria, Illinois, Colorado, LIU, New York University, Oklahoma A&M, and Philadelphia's Temple University—competed for bragging rights. Temple came out on top in the highly successful tournament, defeating Colorado in the final game.

By this time, the coaches and colleges wanted to have more say in the proceedings.

Ohio State coach Harold Olsen made a proposal to the National Association of Basketball Coaches (NABC) that the colleges sponsor their own competition. A new national tournament, slated for March 1939, was authorized by NCAA president William B. Owens. As he stated, "It is entirely fitting that the 'prestige' of college basketball should be supported, and demonstrated to the nation, by the colleges themselves, rather than that this be left to private promotion and enterprise."[24]

The first tournament, won by the University of Oregon, was far from being a success. The NABC lost money, as only 15,025 fans attended the games. Unable to make ends meet, the coaches' group asked the NCAA to take over the tournament. It did so the following year. By the 1950s, the NCAA had overtaken the NIT as the sport's most prestigious postseason tournament. A half century later, it would rank as one of the most watched spectacles in sports.

CHAPTER 4

The Modern-Day Game

BASKETBALL ENTERED THE 1940s with the professional game clearly subordinate to the college product. Few, if any, could have imagined it would eventually take off in popularity and soar to its present heights in the guise of the National Basketball Association (NBA). After many short-lived attempts, it was uncertain whether a professional league could survive at all.

The National Basketball League

In 1935, the Midwest Basketball Conference was established. Paul Sheeks and Frank Kautsky are generally credited with organizing the new circuit, which was based in the Midwest. Rather than being a true league, the conference was nothing more than a loose collection of teams. Some clubs were composed of players employed by a particular company, others were supported by businesses, and still others were independents. The nine teams arranged their own schedules, with a minimum of ten league games required of each. The Chicago Duffy Florals took the league crown the first year, with Ohio's Akron Goodyears winning the championship the second season. The informality of the league was described by Gene Scholz of Ohio's Columbus Athletic Supply squad. "I didn't even know we were in a league," said Scholz. "I was just picking up a few bucks on the side playing basketball."[25]

The following year, the conference changed its name to the National Basketball

League (NBL) in an effort to gain wider national appeal. With several of its teams backed by major corporations, the league managed to remain in existence into the 1940s. When many of its players were called into service during World War II, the league looked to other sources for talent. Ohio's Toledo Jim Whites and Chicago's Studebakers signed several black players, thereby integrating the league.

There were numerous franchise shifts during the decade, but three teams remained relatively stable—Wisconsin's Oshkosh All-Stars and Sheboygan Redskins, and Indiana's Fort Wayne Zollner Pistons. Owned by Fred Zollner, the Pistons implemented a plan that made professional basketball much more attractive to the players. Zollner's players were employed in his piston plant, rather than by the team. After each game, all proceeds from the night's receipts that remained after expenses had been covered were put into a kitty. At the season's conclusion, the money in the kitty was split between the members of the team. The amount each man received made the arrangement quite profitable.

With the end of the war, the league returned to full strength for the 1945–1946 season. A rash of new college stars entered the

The tall and physically gifted George Mikan raised interest in basketball to a new level.

CONTINENTAL BASKETBALL ASSOCIATION

Although most fans have only a passing familiarity with the Continental Basketball Association, it is actually the oldest professional basketball league in the world. It came into existence in 1946, one and a half months before the National Basketball Association (NBA). It was originally known as the Eastern Pennsylvania Basketball League, then later as the Eastern League and the Eastern Basketball Association. Today, it is the only pro league to have formal working agreements with the NBA for both player and referee development.

In the late 1940s, the NBA consisted of eight teams, with 80 players on its rosters. The Eastern League provided a stage for the many good players who were just below NBA caliber. The birth of the American Basketball Association (ABA) in 1967 took many jobs away, and league attendance dropped off significantly. When the NBA added four ABA teams in the 1976 merger, the Eastern League was revitalized. The following year, it took the first step toward nationwide expansion by adding a club in Anchorage, Alaska. Having outgrown its old name, the league became the Continental Basketball Association (CBA) in 1978. As of 2000, it consists of nine teams stretching across the country from Hartford, Connecticut, to Yakima, Washington.

The CBA has provided the NBA with more than five hundred players since it became the official developmental league of the NBA in 1978. Former CBA players who have played in the NBA All-Star Game include Rickey Green, Michael Adams, and John Starks.

league, which expanded its boundaries by adding a team in Rochester, New York. The following season saw further expansion. George Mikan—the first of the game's outstanding tall men—had been added to the roster of the Chicago American Gears at the tail end of the previous season. Mikan raised interest in the game to a new level, as he dominated play unlike anyone before him.

The Basketball Association of America

The teams of the NBL played many of their games in small school gyms. Even these were not filled to capacity in the circuit's early years. By the late 1940s, however, interest in the league had reached new heights. Managers of some of the larger arenas in the country became intrigued by the sport, seeing it as a way to increase profits.

In 1946, several members of the Arena Managers Association of America banded together to form the Basketball Association of America (BAA). Maurice Podoloff was elected the league's first president, and eleven teams—the Boston Celtics, Chicago Stags, Cleveland Rebels, Detroit Falcons, New York Knickerbockers, Philadelphia Warriors, Pittsburgh Ironmen, Providence Steamrollers, St. Louis Bombers, Toronto Huskies, and Washington, D.C., Capitols—initiated the first season of play. Each team played a 60-game schedule, with the Philadelphia Warriors winning the maiden

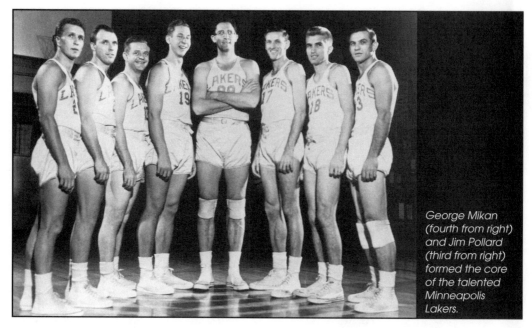

George Mikan (fourth from right) and Jim Pollard (third from right) formed the core of the talented Minneapolis Lakers.

championship. The team was led by Joe Fulks, the first of the great jump-shooters.

Although the first season was a success artistically, it was a failure financially. The franchises in Cleveland, Detroit, Pittsburgh, and Toronto lasted just one season. College basketball remained the number one attraction among fans.

At first, the BAA and NBL managed to coexist on friendly terms. The two leagues agreed not to go after each other's players and discussed a possible playoff series between the champions of the two organizations. By the next year, however, relations had become strained.

Four teams were dropped and a new one added for the BAA's second season. The schedule was reduced to 48 games, with the title being won by the Baltimore Bullets.

Money remained a problem, however, since a shorter schedule meant less income.

In the meantime, the NBL was also experiencing problems. Chicago American Gears owner Maurice White pulled the club—together with the circuit's main drawing card, George Mikan—out of the league, and attempted to found his own association. When the Professional Basketball League of America flopped within weeks, the Gears declared bankruptcy. The NBL distributed the club's players among the remaining teams in the league, with the Minneapolis Lakers awarded Mikan.

With Mikan joining forces with former Stanford star Jim Pollard and several other seasoned pros, Minneapolis had the core of a future dynasty firmly in place. The NBL expanded its schedule to 60 games, and the

Lakers waltzed away with the 1947–1948 league title.

The NBL had six solid franchises and some of the top players in the game. The BAA, however, had a higher growth potential since its teams were housed in larger arenas in major cities. To many, a consolidation of the two leagues seemed an obvious step. The BAA's Podoloff and NBL president Paul Walk held preliminary talks in April 1948 as rumors swirled that four NBL clubs would be jumping to the younger league.

The next month, the BAA announced it was awarding franchises to the Minneapolis, Rochester, Fort Wayne and Indianapolis teams. The remaining NBL owners vowed to fight, threatening to sign BAA players. The BAA responded with promises to retaliate, but little movement between the leagues occurred.

The new teams quickly made their presence felt. Rochester and Minneapolis compiled the top two records in the 1948–1949 season, finishing first and second, respectively, in the league's Western Division. The Lakers, led by scoring champ George Mikan, defeated Chicago, Rochester, and Washington in the playoffs to win the league crown.

The National Basketball Association

Although it was obvious that the BAA had won the war, the NBL refused to close up shop. It awarded four new franchises to replace the ones that had switched leagues and began play for the 1948–1949 season. When the Detroit Vagabond Kings dropped out after winning just 2 of their first 19 games, they were replaced by Ohio's Dayton Rens, descendants of the old New York Renaissance team. With Pop Gates as their coach, the Rens earned the distinction of being the only black team to perform in a white league.

The 1948–1949 season proved to be the NBL's last. In July 1949, a majority of the owners expressed their desire to join forces with the BAA. On August 3, it became official. The BAA accepted seven NBL teams into the fold, giving it a total of seventeen clubs. The name of the league was changed to the National Basketball Association (NBA). (NBA records recognize June 6, 1946—the date the BAA was formed—as the league's official date of birth.)

The NBA faced some immediate problems. Putting together a workable schedule to accommodate seventeen teams was one of the first. The clubs were grouped into three divisions for the first season of play. The Eastern Division consisted of the Baltimore Bullets, Boston Celtics, New York Knickerbockers, Philadelphia Warriors, Syracuse (New York) Nationals, and Washington, D.C., Capitols. The Chicago Stags, Fort Wayne Pistons, Minneapolis Lakers, Rochester Royals, and St. Louis Bombers composed the Central Division. The Western Division included the Anderson (Indiana) Duffey Packers, Denver Nuggets,

Indianapolis Olympians, Sheboygan Redskins, Tri-Cities Blackhawks (representing Moline and Rock Island, Illinois, and Davenport, Iowa), and Waterloo (Iowa) Hawks.

The increased number of teams necessitated a new playoff format. Twelve of the seventeen clubs qualified for postseason play in the 1949–1950 season. The result, however, was the same. With Mikan leading the way, the Lakers won their third successive championship, each one in a different league.

The NBA's growing pains continued through the early years of the 1950s. It quickly became obvious that teams situated in small towns, such as Sheboygan and Waterloo, would have difficulty competing with teams in the major cities. By

the time the 1950–1951 season rolled around, six teams—Chicago, St. Louis, Anderson, Sheboygan, Waterloo, and Denver—had folded. Washington disbanded on January 9, leaving the league with ten franchises.

The following four seasons saw further fine-tuning. In 1951, the Tri-Cities team moved to the larger market of Milwaukee. The Indianapolis Olympians folded in 1953, with the Baltimore Bullets following suit the year after. The 1954–1955 season found the league down to eight teams. Although four of the clubs would relocate to new cities, the league would continue with eight franchises until 1961. At long last, some measure of stability had been arrived at.

THE "LONGEST" GAME

The game played between the Fort Wayne Pistons and the world champion Minneapolis Lakers on November 22, 1950, was not the longest game on record—it just seemed that way. It was the one game most responsible for the adoption of the 24-second rule four years later.

Minneapolis had been nearly invincible on its home court, winning 29 games in a row. The Pistons, on the other hand, had not yet won a game on the road that season. Coach Murray Mendenhall decided a change in strategy was in order.

His plan, simply, was to hold on to the ball as much as possible. By doing so, Fort Wayne was able to take an 8–7 lead after one period of play. The second quarter continued with more of the same, but the Lakers went into their dressing room at halftime with a 13–11 advantage.

The third period ended with Minneapolis holding on to a 17–16 edge. The last quarter saw the teams match single points on free throws, with the Lakers clinging to their slim lead with just seconds remaining. Fort Wayne's Paul Armstrong drove for the basket, then passed off to center Larry Foust. Foust's desperation shot was deflected by George Mikan, but still went in. The Pistons had managed a 19–18 victory in the lowest-scoring game in NBA annals. Mikan scored 15 of his team's 18 points in a losing cause. Guard John Oldham was Fort Wayne's leading scorer with a mere 5 points. As quoted in *Cages to Jump Shots*, Lakers coach John Kundla spoke for most of the owners when he said, "Many more games like that and we can shut up shop."

The integrity of college basketball was undermined when Alex Groza (pictured) and other players were implicated for point shaving.

The College Point-Shaving Scandal of 1951

While the pro leagues struggled to attain respectability, the college game continued to flourish. Part of its appeal was due to the influence of gambling. In the late 1940s, the invention of the point spread made basketball extremely attractive to bettors. It enabled a person to bet on an underdog and win, as long as the team lost by fewer than a previously established number of points. Unfortunately, the large amount of money being bet made controlling the outcome of games an attractive proposition. Rumors surfaced of players being asked to shave points. This meant a player saw to it that his team won by fewer points than expected.

In January 1950, Manhattan College star Junius Kellogg was offered a thousand-dollar bribe to fix the score of a future game against Chicago's DePaul University. He reported the offer to his coach, starting a widespread investigation of over one hundred suspicious games by Manhattan district attorney Frank Hogan. Within a short time, players from Manhattan, Long Island University, the City College of New York, and New York University were accused of shaving points. Coaches from other parts of the country smugly insinuated that the scandal was a New York phenomenon. The big city gamblers "couldn't touch my boys with a ten-foot pole,"[26] bragged Kentucky coach Adolph Rupp.

Sadly, Rupp could not have been more mistaken. Former Kentucky All-Americans Alex Groza and Ralph Beard were caught in the point-shaving web, together with players from Bradley and Toledo. More than thirty players from the seven schools were eventually implicated.

The involvement of City College was especially heartbreaking. The 1949–1950 season had ended with the Beavers winning both the NIT and NCAA tournament—the only time in history that one school won both postseason tournaments in the same year. Their storybook season saw them become the darlings of New York City. The scandal not only prompted the suspension of the basketball program at the school, it also tainted their finest moment. College basketball's image had been tarnished, but the NBA acted quickly. Groza and Beard, now with the Indianapolis Olympians, were immediately banned from the league.

Despite the scandal, college basketball managed to endure. Scoring was on the rise, and stars such as Frank Selvy of South Carolina's Furman University and Tom Gola of Philadelphia's LaSalle University caught the public's fancy. On February 13, 1954, Selvy scored a major-college record of 100 points while leading his club to victory over South Carolina's Newberry College. He averaged 41.7 points per game for the year, yet another mark.

The lure of the easy dollar, however, would always be a temptation for players whose skills might ensure a big payday for gamblers. Occasional cases of point-shaving occurred in the ensuing years, but none of the scope of the 1951 scandal.

The 24-Second Clock

By the early 1950s, the pace of the pro game had slowed down considerably. When teams opened up a lead, they tended to stall in order to use up time. The dominance of George Mikan and the Lakers contributed to the problem. The Rochester Royals won the NBA title in 1951, but Minneapolis came back to take the next three championships. The team's remarkable run gave it a total of six crowns in its first seven years of existence. If opponents had little chance to win, they would sometimes hold on to the ball for long periods of time, figuring their chances would improve if Minneapolis—or any other favorite—was held to fewer shots. Fouling became the only way a team could get possession of the ball. Unfortunately, watching a procession of players march to the foul line held little interest for the fans.

Fearful that their sport was heading down the road to ruin, the owners tried several changes but nothing seemed to work. Finally, Syracuse Nationals owner Danny Biasone had an idea: limit the amount of time that a team had to shoot to 24 seconds. In explaining how he came up with that number, Biasone said, "Teams were taking about 60 shots in a game if nobody screwed around. I figured if the teams combined for 120 shots in a game and the game was 48 minutes long . . . I divided 120 shots into 2,880 seconds. . . . The answer was 24 [seconds]."[27] In the summer of 1954, Biasone invited the other owners to Syracuse for a demonstration of his 24-second rule. They liked what they saw and agreed to try the rule during the upcoming exhibition season. It proved to be such a success that it was immediately adopted for the 1954–1955 regular season.

Another rule change aimed at cutting down the number of fouls. Teams were limited to six personal fouls per quarter. For every one committed after that, the opposing club was awarded an additional free throw. This now made deliberate fouling a less attractive option.

The success of these moves was reflected in a jump in scoring all across the board. The Boston Celtics had led the league in scoring in 1953–1954 with an average of 87.7 points per game. Every club but one surpassed that mark the next season, with the Celtics becoming the first team in history to average over 100 points a contest. Even Boston's Bob Cousy, who used to dribble away the final moments of games when the Celtics were leading, appreciated the rules. "The fouls were getting worse and worse," he recalled. "Guys would really hit you. . . . The clock opened everything up."[28] The NBA had taken a key step in its move toward acceptance as an important major sports league.

Danny Biasone, originator of the twenty-four second clock.

Integration

Although many good black players had been groomed by the colleges, as of 1950 none had appeared in an NBA (or BAA) game. Curiously enough, the success of the Harlem Globetrotters was probably a contributing factor. When Abe Saperstein's team appeared as an opening attraction at NBA arenas, attendance was sure to increase. The owners, not anxious to bite the hand that fed them, were unwilling to hire players who might otherwise go to the Globies. The desire not to alienate white fans undoubtedly added to their reluctance to sign blacks.

In early 1950, Ned Irish of the New York Knickerbockers declared his intention of signing Nat "Sweetwater" Clifton of the Globetrotters. That spring, the Celtics drafted Chuck Cooper in the second round of the league draft. The Capitols followed suit by later selecting Earl Lloyd. On October 31, 1950, Lloyd became the first black to play in a regular-season league game. Cooper followed him the next night, while Clifton—the first of the three to sign a contract—made his debut on November 4. It would be another decade, however, before blacks entered the league in significant numbers. Bill Russell,

Nat "Sweetwater" Clifton (left) and other African Americans broke through the NBA's color barrier in 1950.

TEXAS WESTERN UNIVERSITY VERSUS KENTUCKY

On March 19, 1966, the Miners of Texas Western University took on the Wildcats of Kentucky in the NCAA tournament championship game. Unlike the previous 27 title games, however, this one saw an all-black starting five (Texas Western) matched against an all-white group (Kentucky). It was a landmark game for college basketball.

The contest took on added significance because of Kentucky coach Adolph Rupp's inclination toward all-white recruiting. If the underdog Miners needed any extra incentive, it was provided when coach Don Haskins heard that Rupp reportedly promised that his team would not lose to a club made up of five black players.

The Miners starting five—Bobby Joe Hill, Orsten Artis, Willie Worsley, David Lattin, and Harry Fluornoy—were a group of youngsters familiar with the aggressive, free-spirited, inner-city style of play. Kentucky's starters—known as "Rupp's Runts" since none stood more than six-feet-five-inches tall—were a more disciplined outfit consisting of Thad Jaracz, Tom Kron, Larry Conley, Louis Dampier, and future NBA coaching legend Pat Riley.

Texas Western controlled the game from the opening minutes, but was never able to break it open. Kentucky had numerous chances to apply pressure, but could not make their shots consistently. The Miners prevailed by a score of 72–65, sending Rupp down to defeat in what would be his final chance at a fifth national championship. By the next year, no major college team would ever again rely on recruiting only white players.

Elgin Baylor, Wilt Chamberlain, and Oscar Robertson would be among those in the forefront of the NBA's rise to prominence.

Moving into the Mainstream

George Mikan retired in 1954, signaling the end of the Lakers dynasty. (He did make a brief, ineffective comeback during the 1955–1956 season.) The Boston Celtics were poised to take Minneapolis's place.

Boston coach Red Auerbach's squad included Bob Cousy and Bill Sharman, the best backcourt combination in the league. By obtaining the draft rights to defensive standout Bill Russell in a 1956 trade with the St. Louis Hawks, Auerbach had the vital cog in place. Tom Heinsohn and Frank Ramsey also joined the team that year, and the Celtics won their first championship. The game which gave them the title was a double-overtime thriller in Game 7 of the NBA Finals against St. Louis. With a large television audience watching, the league had taken a giant step forward in its quest for national recognition.

After a one-year intermission, the Celtics won the next eight crowns in a row, and ten of the next eleven. Their fast-breaking style, keyed by Russell's explosive outlet passes, made them the undisputed class of the league.

Other blacks brought their distinctive styles to the game, too. Elgin Baylor took his acrobatic, high-flying moves to the Lakers; Oscar Robertson controlled games for Cincinnati with his all-around brilliance; and Wilt Chamberlain dominated action around the basket with the Philadelphia Warriors and 76ers, setting scoring and rebounding marks unlikely ever to be matched. Chamberlain's memorable battles with Russell were an important factor in helping the NBA obtain a national television contract.

As the league gained popularity, it began to expand its operations on an almost yearly basis. The Lakers moved west to Los Angeles in 1960, Chicago joined the league in 1961, and the Warriors moved to San Francisco in 1962. Walter Kennedy replaced Maurice Podoloff as commissioner the next year and watched the Chicago Stags move to Baltimore and the Syracuse Nationals replace the Warriors in Philadelphia. No further changes took place until Chicago rejoined the league in 1966 as the Bulls. The next year saw Seattle and San Diego awarded franchises, followed by Milwaukee and Phoenix in 1968. The NBA had nearly doubled in size in less than a decade, and further expansion was being planned.

One person upset with the Lakers' move to Los Angeles in 1960 was Abe Saperstein. The league had denied the Globetrotters' owner a franchise on the West Coast prior to the Lakers' shift. With professional basketball becoming more established, Saperstein decided to start his own league, in part to get even with the NBA. The result was the American Basketball League (ABL), which began play in 1961 with eight teams and Saperstein as commissioner.

The new circuit did not pose a threat to the older league and folded after just a year and a half. It did, however, introduce an interesting new twist to the game. The ABL awarded 3 points for any shot taken from a distance of twenty-five feet or more. Six years later, the 3-point shot would be resurrected by another challenger to NBA dominance—the American Basketball Association.

The American Basketball Association

With interest in the NBA at an all-time high, the American Basketball Association (ABA) entered the picture in 1967. Realizing the need for attracting attention, the eleven-team circuit named NBA legend George Mikan as its commissioner. To make the game more appealing, it revived the ABL's 3-point shot, and introduced a flashy red-white-and-blue ball. Many longtime NBA observers laughed at the latter. "That ball belongs on the nose of a seal,"[29] sneered Philadelphia coach Alex Hannum.

The 3-point shot extended defenses in the new league. This allowed the more athletic players to display their talents to the fullest extent. This playground style of play attracted many new fans into ABA arenas. The wide-open style was a harbinger of things to come in the NBA.

One of the most spectacular of this new generation of players was Julius Erving, nicknamed "Dr. J." He played his game "above the rim," soaring through the air on his drives toward the basket and slamming home thunderous, crowd-pleasing dunks. No one had ever before seen such gravity-defying maneuvers. Almost single-handedly, Erving gave the ABA credibility.

By 1975, despite having some of pro basketball's most exciting players under contract, the ABA was in serious trouble. Salaries had skyrocketed, and without a national television contract, several clubs were experiencing severe financial problems. The disastrous 1975–1976 season proved to be the upstart league's last. Owners struggled to meet payrolls, and attendance dropped precipitously. "Every day was a crisis,"[30] remembered former New York Knickerbockers star Dave DeBusschere, the seventh—and last—commissioner of the league.

On June 17, 1976, an agreement was reached between the two leagues. The Denver Nuggets, Indiana Pacers, New York Nets, and San Antonio Spurs each paid $3.2 million to become members of the NBA, raising the total number of teams in the league to twenty-two. The influx of players gave the league an injection of badly needed new blood. Julius Erving, Moses Malone, George Gervin, Maurice Lucas, David Thompson, and Dan Issel were a few of the ABA stars who now had a chance to show how they could do in direct competition with proven NBA commodities like Kareem Abdul-Jabbar, Pete Maravich, Bob McAdoo, Bill Walton, and Elvin Hayes. The result was a more entertaining product for professional basketball fans. It would become even more appealing three years later when the league adopted the 3-point shot for the 1979–1980 season.

Julius Erving's high-flying acrobatics brought credibility to the ABA.

The UCLA Dynasty

Many NBA stars of the 1970s were linked by a common thread. Kareem Abdul-Jabbar, Bill Walton, Gail Goodrich, Keith Wilkes,

Sidney Wicks, Walt Hazzard, Henry Bibby, Keith Erickson, Swen Nater, Lucius Allen, Curtis Rowe, David Meyers, and Marques Johnson were members of the greatest college dynasty of all time. They all played for John Wooden—known as the "Wizard of Westwood"—at the University of California at Los Angeles (UCLA), and, incredibly, all won national championships.

UCLA dominated college basketball like no other team had, before or since. From 1964 to 1975, the UCLA Bruins won ten national titles in twelve years, including seven in a row. No other school has won more than seven championships, or more than two consecutively. Four times (in 1964, 1967, 1972, and 1973) Wooden's squads compiled perfect 30–0 records.

Wooden accomplished this with a variety of teams. He won with big men at center, with high-scoring forwards, and with small teams dominated by the guard positions. His twenty-seven years at UCLA saw his teams win 620 games while losing only 147. From January 30, 1971, through January 17, 1974, the Bruins won an amazing 88 consecutive games for an all-time record.

Largely thanks to Wooden and UCLA, the NCAA tournament grew by leaps and bounds. The Final Four—the semifinal and final round games of the tournament —became firmly established as one of the country's most-watched sporting events. With national television coverage, it gave some of the game's greatest players a setting in which to put their talents on display before the entire country. None took greater advantage of that opportunity than Magic Johnson and Larry Bird.

The 1980s

By the end of the 1970s, pro basketball was showing signs of slipping. The last three championships of the decade had been won by teams located in Portland, Washington, D.C., and Seattle. Franchises in the league's three most important markets—New York, Los Angeles, and Boston—were struggling along with mediocre clubs. Aside from Julius Erving, there was no player who captured the imagination of fans everywhere. Adding to the disenchantment of many fans were the widespread rumors of drug abuse among NBA stars.

Such was the atmosphere as Michigan State and Indiana State prepared to face off for college basketball's national championship in the 1979 NCAA tournament. Michigan was led by a charismatic six-foot-nine-inch guard named Earvin "Magic" Johnson. Indiana's star was six-foot-nine-inch college Player of the Year Larry Bird from the tiny town of French Lick, Indiana. The matchup received national attention, and more than 25 million viewers tuned in to see the two All-Americans do battle. It was the largest viewing audience in the history of basketball—either college or pro.

Johnson led Michigan State to a 75–64 victory over the previously unbeaten Sycamores, as interest in college basketball reached its zenith. When Johnson and Bird entered the NBA that fall, the league received a shot in the arm. Bird joined the Celtics and sparked the club to a 32-game improvement over its record of the previous season. Boston jumped from last place in the NBA's Atlantic Division to first. Johnson was welcomed by Abdul-Jabbar and company in Los Angeles. The Lakers, who finished third in the Pacific Division in 1979, improved by 13 games and won the division title in 1980. In the playoffs, Magic sparked his team to wins over Phoenix, Seattle, and Philadelphia, giving the Lakers their first championship since 1972.

Bird and Johnson became perennial All-Stars, leading their teams to one champi-

onship after another. Either Boston or Los Angeles won the NBA title in eight of the pair's first nine seasons in the league. More importantly, they revived interest in the professional game, showing millions of fans how the game should be played.

In the early years of the decade, the NBA finalized negotiations with both ESPN and the USA network to broadcast games on cable. David Stern, in charge of marketing the league, helped bring the deals to fruition. He would later play an important role in shoring up the game's image and popularizing it around the world as commissioner. He received a good bit of help from a young man out of the University of North Carolina—Michael Jordan.

Michigan State guard Earvin "Magic" Johnson (left) and Indiana State forward Larry Bird at a press conference before their teams' famed match up in 1979.

The Jordan Era

The year 1984 marked the long-awaited first meeting of Bird's Celtics and Johnson's Lakers in the NBA finals. Boston came out on top in a thrilling series, winning 4 games to 3. Game 7 set records by attracting more television viewers than any other game in NBA history.

Shortly after the series ended, the league held its annual draft. The Chicago Bulls, picking third, selected Michael Jordan, a six-foot-five-inch guard who had led the North Carolina Tar Heels to the NCAA title in 1982.

Jordan broke into the league in spectacular fashion, finishing third in scoring and winning Rookie of the Year honors. He sat out most of his second season with a broken foot but came back in time for the playoffs. The Bulls were swept by Boston in their first-round series, but Jordan put on a show. He scored 131 points in the three contests, including a playoff record 63 points in Game 2.

The next year saw Jordan win the first of seven consecutive scoring titles, solidifying his status as the game's most exciting player. Despite the individual honors that came his way, he was far from satisfied. In his first six seasons, the Bulls never finished higher than second place in the NBA's Central Division.

Jordan's frustration finally ended in 1991. Chicago won its first NBA title, then repeated as champs in 1992 and 1993. Following a brief retirement during which he tried his hand at professional baseball, Jordan returned to the NBA wars and led the Bulls to three more championships (1996,

Chicago Bulls shooting guard Michael Jordan, one of the game's most prolific scorers.

1997, and 1998). The six titles in eight seasons place the Bulls behind only the Celtics in terms of NBA dynasties.

Jordan's influence on basketball was not limited to his play on the court. His acrobatic style and love for the game won him legions of fans around the world, while his universal appeal gave the NBA unimagined exposure. He was the perfect athlete to bring the league to glory. As his agent, David Falk, said, "If you were to create a media athlete, and star for the '90s—spectacular talent, midsized, well-spoken, attractive, accessible, old-time values, wholesome, clean, natural, not too goody-two-shoes, with a little bit of deviltry in him—you'd invent Michael."[31]

Basketball enters the twenty-first century at the height of its popularity. A new generation of superstars stands ready to carry the torch that has been passed to them by Jordan. It remains open to conjecture whether Shaquille O'Neal, Grant Hill, Kevin Garnett, Allen Iverson, Kobe Bryant, Stephon Marbury, or anyone else can fill Jordan's sneakers. What is certain, however, is that millions of youngsters on courts around the globe dream of getting the chance to try.

CHAPTER 5

Superstars One and All

IT IS IRONIC that basketball—a game in which a club's success is so dependent on teamwork—owes a major part of its appeal to individual superstars. The "one-on-one" play popularized on playgrounds across the country has become more and more intrinsic to the pro game. A player who can dominate in just one area can dictate whether a team succeeds or fails at the box office.

George Mikan

Long before there was Michael Jordan, there was George Mikan. Mikan was basketball's first superstar, a six-foot-ten-inch giant who towered over opponents and dominated the game. His status was reflected in the message that adorned the marquee outside Madison Square Garden when Mikan's

Lakers played the hometown Knickerbockers in 1950: "TONITE: GEO. MIKAN VS. KNICKS."[32]

The original "Mr. Basketball," Mikan was a gawky Illinois farm boy who entertained thoughts of becoming a priest. He attended DePaul University in Illinois, where coach Ray Meyer took him under his wing. Mikan began to flourish. His domination of the college game was so great that he was in part responsible for the introduction of the rule banning goaltending in 1944.

Following his graduation, Mikan signed with the Chicago Gears of the NBL, and led them to a title in 1947. When the team folded, Mikan went to the Minneapolis Lakers in a special dispersal draft. Teaming up with Vern Mikkelsen, Jim Pollard, Slater

Martin, and Whitey Skoog, he helped make the Lakers almost unbeatable. Over the next seven seasons, Minneapolis won the last World Tournament (1947), an NBL title (1948), a BAA championship (1949), and four NBA crowns (1950, 1952, 1953, 1954). Along the way, Mikan won three scoring titles, one rebounding crown, and a Most Valuable Player (MVP) award.

Mikan's play inspired the NBA to widen the foul lanes in 1951–1952. Three years later, it instituted the 24-second clock, partly in order to prevent opposing teams from stalling in an attempt to keep the Lakers from getting possession of the ball. Mikan's impact on the game was such that in 1950 the Associated Press named him the "Greatest Player of the First Half-Century."

Big George's influence did not end with his retirement. He became the first commissioner of the ABA, and was responsible for the idea of using the red-white-and-blue ball.

Bob Cousy

Known as the "Houdini of the Hardwood," Bob Cousy brought a splash of showmanship to the NBA that had not been seen before. His behind-the-back passes brought fans to their feet as he guided the Boston Celtics to one world title after another. Had it not been for a bit

of luck, however, Cousy would have performed his magic for another NBA team.

After an All-American career at Massachusetts' College of the Holy Cross, Cousy was selected by the Tri-Cities Blackhawks in the first round of the 1950 NBA draft. Almost immediately, the Blackhawks traded him to the Chicago Stags. Unfortunately, the Chicago franchise soon folded, and the league held a special dispersal draft for Stags players. With only three players left—rookie Cousy and veterans Max Zaslofsky and

Bob Cousy brought fans to their feet with his basketball showmanship.

Bill Russell, seen here putting up a hook shot, possessed the ability to take over a game with his defense.

Andy Phillip—the names were placed in a hat. (No one, it seems, wanted Cousy.) When the two veterans were selected first, Boston was left with the crowd-pleasing playmaker, much to coach Red Auerbach's annoyance. "Am I supposed to win," he once asked, "or please the local yokels?"[33]

It did not take Auerbach long, however, to realize what he had in Cousy. In addition to averaging more than 18 points per game for his fourteen seasons, the "Cooz" also led the NBA in assists for eight consecutive years. He once passed off for 28 baskets in a game, a record at the time. In 1953, he scored 50 points in a quadruple-overtime playoff victory over the Syracuse Nationals. He connected on 30 free throws, a mark still on the books nearly fifty years later.

Bill Russell

In 1980, the Professional Basketball Writers' Association of America named Bill Russell as the Greatest Player in the History of the NBA. This might seem surprising if only individual statistics were examined. The only category in which Russell ever led the league was in rebounds, a total of four times.

Statistics can be misleading, however. What they do not show is the intensity with which Russell played. He was the only player who could control a game with his defense, without scoring so much as a single point. Former NBA star Jack Twyman described what opposing players had to look forward to when they played the Celtics. "Russell was the greatest impact player in any sport," said Twyman. "You knew that if you got by Cousy or Heinsohn . . . Russell was back there waiting to block your shot. No one ever dominated a sport the way Russell did with the Celtics."[34]

Had blocked shots been an official statistic in those days, Russell surely would have set the standard for years to come. He did not bat balls into the stands, allowing the opposition to regain possession. Instead, he controlled the ball either by hitting it to a teammate or by catching it himself. The result was usually another easy Boston basket off their trademark fast break. Opponents became acutely aware of his presence. "Bill put a whole new sound in pro basketball," explained his coach, Red Auerbach, "the sound of his footsteps."[35]

The only thing that really matters in sports is winning, and Bill Russell was the ultimate winner. At the University of San Francisco, he led his squad to national titles in both 1955 and 1956. After graduating, he won a gold medal as a member of the U.S. team at the 1956 Olympics in Melbourne, Australia. (He also qualified for the Games as a high jumper, but declined the chance to compete.) Turning pro that fall, his professional career saw him win an incredible eleven championships in thirteen years, the final two as a player/coach. Equally notable, he was also the first black coach in NBA history.

Perhaps one final statistic stands out as the perfect example of Russell's—and the Celtics'—status as sport's ultimate winner. During his thirteen years with the team,

there were fourteen occasions when the Celtics faced one game they had to win, or else lose and go home. In each and every one of those contests, Russell and the Celtics were victorious.

Wilt Chamberlain

Wilt Chamberlain was the most dominating player the game of basketball has ever seen. Standing seven feet one inch and weighing close to three hundred pounds, he stood out as a giant among men. Wilt appeared to be able to do whatever he wanted on the court, whenever he wanted to do it. While playing

Wilt Chamberlain, basketball's most dominating force.

for the Philadelphia Warriors, he led the NBA in scoring seven consecutive seasons, averaging an incredible 50.4 points per game during the 1961–1962 campaign. He scored a single-game record 100 points in a contest against New York that year, surprising even himself. "When I made my first nine free throws," he later recalled, "I thought I'd be heading for some kind of foul-shooting record. But never in my fondest dreams did I ever expect I would score a hundred points going into that game."[36]

Chamberlain also led the league in rebounding eleven times. His single-game high of 55 is another NBA record, as is his lifetime average of nearly 23 rebounds per game. When criticized for shooting too much, he took it upon himself to silence his critics. The result saw him lead the league in assists in 1967–1968.

While playing for the Los Angeles Lakers in 1972, Wilt was the cornerstone of a team that ran off a professional sports record of 33 consecutive victories. The

BEVO FRANCIS

In the early 1950s, Rio Grande College was a tiny school nestled in the southeastern corner of Ohio, with an enrollment of just ninety-two students. Thirty-eight of them were male, and eleven of those played on the school's basketball team. One of the eleven—Clarence "Bevo" Francis—was responsible for lifting the school into the national sports headlines.

The six-foot-nine-inch Francis was one of the greatest pure shooters of all time. In his freshman year, he shattered nearly every scoring record in existence. He scored 1,954 points (50.1 per game) on 708 field goals and 538 free throws while leading Rio Grande to a perfect 39–0 mark. In one game, against Ashland Junior College, Bevo scored an unbelievable 116 points.

Unfortunately, the NCAA disallowed his records that summer. It ruled that records must be set while playing a schedule made up mostly of four-year, degree-awarding institutions. Many of Rio Grande's opponents were junior colleges and military bases.

The next year, the school played a stronger schedule, including games against Providence College, Pennsylvania's Villanova University, North Carolina's Wake Forest University, and North Carolina State. Francis continued to score at will, averaging 47 points per contest. Included was another triple-digit scoring effort. The Rio Grande Redmen defeated Michigan's Hillsdale College, 134–91, with Bevo pouring in 113 points. He scored 38 field goals that night, hitting his turnaround jumper from all angles, and 37 of 42 free throws. His record still remains a single-game standard nearly half a century later.

An injury ended Bevo's college career, and he left school after his sophomore year. He toured with the Harlem Globetrotters as a member of the Boston Whirlwinds, one of the teams that barnstormed with them. In 1956, he turned down an offer to play with the Philadelphia Warriors of the NBA in order to stay closer to home with his wife and family.

Lakers won the NBA title that season, giving Chamberlain his second championship. He won his first as a member of the Philadelphia 76ers in 1967.

Chamberlain's athletic talents were not limited to basketball. He was a standout track and field athlete in high school, and probably could have excelled at any sport he turned his attention to. On the court, however, he was in a class by himself.

Jerry West

Many modern-day fans, being too young to have seen Jerry West play, recognize him as the highly successful general manager of the Los Angeles Lakers. Without realizing it, however, they have seen the form displayed by one of the greatest shooters of all time on many occasions. For the past quarter century, the official logo of the NBA has been a silhouette of a player dribbling a ball in perfect form. The perfect form is that of Jerry West.

West made a name for himself as a scoring star at West Virginia. He joined the Lakers in 1960 and molded a Hall of Fame career over the next thirteen seasons. Today, more than a quarter century after having played his last game, West's 27.0 career scoring average is fifth on the all-time list. With his career overlapping that of Wilt

Jerry West's ability to excel at key moments in a game earned him the nickname "Mr. Clutch."

Chamberlain, however, West won only one scoring title.

West also won only one championship in his career, through no fault of his own. His playoff scoring average surpassed his regular-season mark, as he poured through just over 29 points per game for 153 contests. In 1965, the Lakers fell to the Celtics despite West's averaging 40.6 points for 11 playoff games, and an incredible 46.3 for the 5 games of the Finals series. His ability to come through when most needed gave

THE 1972 U.S. OLYMPIC TEAM

Basketball became an official Olympic sport in Berlin in 1936. (Previously, it had been a demonstration sport in the 1904 Games in St. Louis.) The United States swept all of its games to win the gold medal that year, and proceeded to do the same in each of the next six Olympiads. The U.S. team's undefeated streak would end unceremoniously in the 1972 competition in Munich. Most observers consider the game that ended the streak to be among the most blatant thefts in sports history.

The gold medal game of that twentieth Olympiad saw the U.S. team matched against the Soviet Union. Leading for much of the contest, the Soviets led 49–48 with just six seconds left and the ball in their possession. U.S. guard Doug Collins intercepted a pass, drove to the basket, and was fouled. He connected on both free throws to give the Americans their first lead of the game, 50–49. The events of the next three seconds are hard to comprehend.

As the second shot left Collins' hands, the Soviets called time out. This was disallowed, since international rules mandated that time could not be called until the ball was inbounded. Soviet players from the bench raced onto the court in protest, causing a stoppage of play with one second remaining on the clock.

When play resumed, the Soviet inbounds passer stepped on the line, but no call was made. He hurled a long pass that was batted away, apparently giving the victory to the United States. Incredibly, however, with no authority to do so, the secretary general of the International Amateur Basketball Federation came down from the stands and overruled the officials. The Soviets were granted their time-out, and three seconds were put back on the clock.

With yet another chance, the Soviets prepared to inbound the ball. The referee ordered U.S. defender Tom McMillen to step back in order to give Ivan Edeshko more room, enforcing a rule that does not exist in international play. Edeshko threw another court-length pass. It was caught by Aleksandr Belov, who proceeded to get around two defenders and score the winning basket—all in less than three seconds. The U.S. streak had ended in one of the most bizarre finishes to a basketball game anyone had ever seen.

As a matter of principle, the Americans voted to boycott the awards ceremony and refuse their medals. Those medals remain in a bank vault in Switzerland.

A Russian and U.S. player battle for the ball during the 1972 Olympic Games.

him the nickname of "Mr. Clutch." One of the most famous baskets in NBA history was his 60-foot shot at the buzzer in Game 3 of the 1970 NBA Finals series against the New York Knickerbockers. The shot tied the game, which the Lakers eventually lost in overtime. Had the 3-point rule been in effect, the shot would have given Los Angeles the victory.

Oscar Robertson

Oscar Robertson's talents were perhaps best summed up by Celtics coach Red Auerbach. "There is nothing he can't do," said Auerbach. "No one comes close to him or has the ability to break open a game as Oscar. He's so great he scares me. He can beat you all by himself and usually does."[37]

The man he was talking about was considered by many to be the perfect basketball player. The "Big O," as he was called, combined a great shooting touch with superb ball-handling skills and unsurpassed court presence. He moved as if he had the ball attached to his hand by a string, never losing his composure no matter what the situation.

The six-foot-five-inch Robertson was a three-time All-American in college at Cincinnati, and a twelve-time All-Star in the pros. He averaged better than 30 points a game six times in his NBA career, and led in assists per game eight times. Nowadays, players make headlines when they record a triple-double (reaching double figures in a game in three separate categories). During

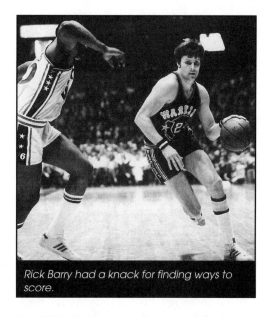

Rick Barry had a knack for finding ways to score.

the 1961–1962 season, the twenty-four-year-old Robertson averaged a triple-double for the entire season, the only time it has ever been done. In seventy-nine games, he averaged 30.8 points, 11.4 assists, and 12.5 rebounds per contest. When that 1962 season is combined with the previous one and the following three, Robertson averaged a triple-double for the five-year span (30.3 points, 10.6 assists, 10.4 rebounds). Although he was not as flashy or acrobatic as Michael Jordan, Robertson is still considered by many to be the greatest all-around basketball player ever to play the game.

Rick Barry

Modern-day fans of the NBA are familiar with the name Barry. Brent and Jon Barry have each spent time in the league, experiencing varying degrees of success. The most

JACK MOLINAS

Jack Molinas should have been a superstar in the National Basketball Association. His talent and intelligence should have guaranteed him a bright future. Unfortunately, his name lives on only in infamy.

Growing up in the Bronx, Molinas was an honor student and standout player at Stuyvesant High School in New York City. He attended Columbia University, where he was an All-American as a six-foot-six-inch forward. His greed, however, led him down the path to ruin. He was convinced he could outsmart anyone and get away with anything.

During college, Molinas had been guilty of shaving points. He escaped detection in the 1951 basketball betting scandal and eventually was the first-round choice of the Fort Wayne Zollner Pistons in the 1954 NBA draft. His rookie season saw him average 12 points per game, and he was a member of the squad picked to play in the All-Star Game. Just prior to the game, however, Molinas admitted to having bet on his team. In accordance with league rules, he was suspended from the NBA for life.

Molinas entered law school and became an attorney. He kept his hand in sports, using his contacts to help him fix college games. He was eventually implicated in the 1961 basketball scandal. He was convicted of conspiracy and bribery and served four years in prison.

After his release, Molinas moved to Los Angeles, where he became involved in several businesses, including one dealing with the distribution of pornographic films. His gambling got him deeply in debt and caused him to make enemies. On August 3, 1975, forty-three-year-old Jack Molinas was shot dead in what is believed to have been a mob-related hit.

famous Barry of all, however, is the patriarch of the clan, Rick Barry, voted one of the NBA's 50 Greatest Players of All Time.

Barry was a basketball maverick. After playing with the San Francisco Warriors for two seasons, he jumped to the fledgling ABA. A court ruling, however, forced him to sit out a year before joining his father-in-law, general manager Bruce Hale, on the Oakland Oaks. After four successful seasons in the new league, he returned to the NBA, rejoining the Warriors.

Though not a pure shooter, Barry was one of the greatest scorers in basketball history. He was the ultimate basketball "garbage man," always finding a way to put the ball into the basket. He did so often enough to become the only man in history to win scoring titles in the NCAA, the ABA, and the NBA. For his pro career, he scored over 25,000 points in fourteen seasons, or an average of nearly 25 points per game. By leading the NBA in scoring in 1967, he ended Wilt Chamberlain's streak of seven consecutive scoring titles.

The native of New Jersey was also an outstanding passer, and arguably the best ever from the foul line. He made 90 percent of his attempts as the last of the underhand free-throw shooters.

Kareem Abdul-Jabbar

Sometimes basketball phenoms fizzle out, never attaining the stardom predicted for them. Such was definitely not the case with Ferdinand Lewis Alcindor Jr.

As a seven-foot-tall high school standout in New York City, Alcindor was one of the most highly publicized prep players ever. He led Power Memorial High to a 116–1 record before moving on to UCLA. His domination of the college game was so great, the NCAA instituted a "no-dunk" rule in an effort to limit his effectiveness. By the time his college career was over, Alcindor had led the Bruins to three NCAA titles, won Player of the Year honors two times, and won an unprecedented three NCAA tournament MVP awards.

After graduation, Alcindor embraced the religion of Islam. He changed his name to Kareem Abdul-Jabbar following the 1970–1971 season as he continued his domination in the pro ranks. In the first year of what would be a remarkable twenty-year NBA career, he won Rookie of the Year honors as he helped the Milwaukee Bucks improve their record of the previous year by 29 games. The next season, the Bucks won the NBA title, the first of six championships for Abdul-Jabbar. Most of his success—and the remaining five of his titles—came with the Los Angeles Lakers. By the time he retired, Abdul-Jabbar had six MVP trophies on his mantel, together with a host of other awards. He finished his career as the NBA's all-time leading scorer, with a total of 38,387 points to his credit. He also ranks number three in rebounds and number two

in blocked shots. His ability to dominate a game was summed up by Bob Cousy, at the time the coach of the Cincinnati Royals. "They can talk theory all they want," said Cousy, "but if [he] comes to play, we can just go home."[38]

Pete Maravich

Quite simply, Pete Maravich was the greatest scorer in the history of college basketball. He is the only major college player to average better than a point a minute for his entire career. "Pistol Pete," as he was nicknamed, led the nation in scoring in each of his three varsity seasons at Louisiana State University (LSU), totaling 3,667 points, or 44.2 per game. Had today's rules been in effect, his totals would have been even higher, since many of his shots were launched from well beyond the 3-point line. Luckily, he did not have to worry about shot selection: his coach at LSU was his father, Press Maravich.

Maravich's shot making was matched only by his magical ball handling and ability as a showman. His passes emerged from behind his back, under his arm, or between his legs, often taking his teammates by complete surprise. Legend has it that he developed his dribbling skills as a youngster by bringing a basketball with him when he went to the movies. He would sit in an aisle seat so he could practice dribbling while watching the screen.

As a pro, Maravich continued his high-scoring ways. While playing for the New

Orleans Jazz, he led the NBA in scoring in the 1976–1977 season, and he was an All-Star on five occasions. Sadly, however, his talents never translated into a championship, either in college or in the pros.

Maravich's story ended far too soon. He died of a heart attack at the age of forty while playing an informal pickup game of basketball.

Julius Erving

Michael Jordan became famous for his gravity-defying moves on the court. None of his moves, however, were any more acrobatic than those of "Doctor J," Julius Erving. Erving brought showmanship to the NBA, electrifying crowds with his athletic prowess.

Upon leaving the University of Massachusetts following his junior year, Erving signed with the Virginia Squires of the ABA. After two years, he moved on to the New York Nets. He carried the Nets to two league championships, in 1974 and 1976, winning MVP honors both seasons.

More than just carrying his team, Erving effectively carried the entire league. His crowd-pleasing style and thunderous dunks were important factors leading to the merger between the NBA and ABA in 1976. As his former coach Kevin Loughery put it, "I honestly believe that Doc did more for pro basketball than anybody, on or off the court. He wasn't just the franchise with the Nets—he was the league."[39]

Following a salary dispute, Erving was sold to the Philadelphia 76ers. He played eleven seasons with Philadelphia, garnering MVP honors in 1981 and helping his team to the championship two years later.

One of the most memorable moments of Erving's career did not take place during a game. At the 1976 ABA All-Star Game festivities, he won the league's slam dunk competition. His winning move brought everyone to their feet as he took off from the foul line, soared through the air, and slammed the ball home through the hoop. The dunk shot would never be the same.

Larry Bird

Most basketball experts agree that Larry Bird was the greatest forward ever to play the game. At six feet nine inches in height, he was perhaps the finest long-distance shooter of all time for his size, regularly draining shots from beyond the 3-point line. In fact, Bird captured the first three NBA All-Star Saturday Long Distance Shootout trophies.

It was his pinpoint passing and overall court sense, however, which separated him from all other forwards. Bird had the intelligence and skills to run a game, like a point guard, from the forward position. These skills were recognized and appreciated by Celtics general manager Red Auerbach. "If I had to start a team," said Auerbach, "the one guy in all history I would take would be Larry. He's the greatest to ever play the game."[40] This came from the man who coached Bill Rus-

Larry Bird releases a long-range jump shot during a game against his team's rival, the Lakers.

sell, Bob Cousy, and John Havlicek, among others.

Bird burst onto the basketball scene when he led his Indiana State squad to the number one spot in the 1979 college polls. In the NCAA finals that season, the Sycamores lost a thriller to Magic Johnson's Michigan State team. The game marked the beginning of a rivalry that would entertain fans throughout the next decade. Bird's Celtics and Johnson's Lakers would meet in the NBA Finals on three occasions, with Boston taking the title in 1984, and Los Angeles in 1985 and 1987.

A bad back finally forced Bird into retirement in 1992. His thirteen NBA seasons saw him score just under 22,000 points (24.3 per contest), grab nearly 9,000 rebounds (10.0), and dole out just shy of 5,700 assists (6.4). He won three championship rings with Boston, three MVP awards, and nine consecutive elections to the All-NBA first team. Perhaps more importantly, Bird, together with Johnson, helped the NBA reach the height of its popularity.

Magic Johnson

Magic Johnson redefined the position of point guard. Never before had a six-foot-nine-inch player (the same height as Bill

Russell) led his team from that vital spot. "Magic is aware of everybody," said Lakers assistant coach Bill Bertka. "Magic sees everything, and he understands everything he sees."[41]

Johnson's ability to play any position on the court was best illustrated in Game 6 of the 1980 NBA Finals series between the Los Angeles Lakers and the Philadelphia 76ers. Kareem Abdul-Jabbar was sidelined by an injury, so the rookie Johnson started at center. Playing every position on the court at one time or another, Johnson led the Lakers to victory by scoring 42 points, pulling down 15 rebounds, and handing out 7 assists. For his all-around performance, Johnson was named MVP of the Finals, the first of three such awards he would win.

That season marked the beginning of one of the greatest all-around careers in NBA annals. Johnson's contagious smile and inspired play helped give a tremendous boost to the league's fortunes in the 1980s. By the time he was forced to retire in 1991 after becoming infected with the AIDS virus, the NBA had seen its popularity soar, in large part because of Johnson.

Like other all-time greats, Johnson's play helped bring out the best in his teammates. He led the Lakers

to five championships during the 1980s, establishing himself as the game's best all-around player since Oscar Robertson. He ended his career with averages of 19.5 points, 11.1 assists, and 7.2 rebounds per game, and numerous playoff marks. As Julius Erving once explained, "He's the only player who can take only three shots and still dominate a game."[42]

Los Angeles Lakers guard Magic Johnson redefined the point guard position.

Michael Jordan

Michael Jordan was arguably the greatest basketball player ever to lace on a pair of sneakers. He rewrote several chapters of the record book, and in the process emerged as the wealthiest, most recognized athlete in the world—all this for a player who was cut from his high school basketball team as a sophomore. Rather than giving up, Jordan honed his skills and improved his game. By the time he entered the University of North Carolina, coach Dean Smith knew he had something special.

Jordan became one of the few freshmen ever to start for Smith. His basket in the final seconds of the championship game that year gave the Tar Heels the national title. He won Player of the Year honors in both his sophomore and junior years, then was selected by the Chicago Bulls with the third pick of the 1984 NBA draft.

Jordan won the Rookie of the Year award in 1985, averaging over 28 points a game. His third year saw him average 37.1 points—the sixth-highest single-season mark in league history—for the first of his record ten scoring titles. With Jordan leading the way, the Bulls won the NBA championship in 1991, then repeated the next two seasons. The following year, he shocked the basketball world by announcing he was retiring in order to play professional baseball. After seventeen months, he returned to the NBA and picked up where he left off. He led Chicago to

Michael Jordan, arguably the NBA's greatest player, is the most recognized athlete in the world.

three more titles before finally retiring for good in 1998.

The record Jordan left is unmatched. He has the highest career scoring average in league history (31.4), the highest career playoff scoring average (33.4), and the second-highest number of 50-plus-point games, trailing only Wilt Chamberlain. He won five MVP awards and six NBA Finals MVP awards. He also starred on defense, where he led the league in steals on three occasions, and was a perennial member of the NBA All-Defensive First Team. A testament to his all-around excellence is the fact that he is the only scoring champion to also win Defensive Player of the Year honors (1988).

Apart from the numbers, Jordan will always be remembered as the supreme "above the rim" player. His artistic moves and spectacular dunks will never be forgotten by those who saw them. He was the ultimate clutch player, always anxious to take the final shot when the game was on the line. More often than not, he made that shot. He was, truly, a performer without equal.

John Stockton

The 1984 NBA draft produced superstars Michael Jordan, Hakeem Olajuwon, and Charles Barkley. A less-publicized player who came out that year has become a dominant playmaker from the point guard position. John Stockton of Gonzaga College was chosen by the Utah Jazz with the sixteenth overall pick. Since becoming a starter in his third year, Stockton has gone on to enter his name in the record books with one assist mark after another.

Utah Jazz point guard John Stockton is basketball's all-time career leader in assists.

In 1988, he collected 1,128 assists to break the single-season record, then surpassed his own standard two times in the next three years. He has topped the NBA in that category a record nine straight seasons, from 1988 through 1996. Included are seven seasons with 1,000 or more assists. Only two other players have reached that total in a season even once. Along the way, Stockton passed Magic Johnson to become the league's all-time career leader. He also tops the charts in average number of assists per game in both single-season and career listings.

Stockton's talents are not limited to passing the ball. He is an excellent shooter, as witnessed by his 52 percent career field-goal percentage and career mark of better than 13 points per game. The native of Spokane, Washington, has also shone on defense. He stands first on the all-time steals list, with more than 2,500 to his credit.

Although he is often overshadowed by flashier players, his talents are appreciated by his peers. "He's the best," said All-Star guard Gary Payton. "When I came into the league, he was the guy who took me to school. I'm still looking for a weakness in his game."[43]

Dennis Rodman

Dennis Rodman is the most tattooed, body-pierced, hair-dyed, outrageous player in the history of basketball. He is also one of the greatest rebounders the game has ever seen. The six-foot-eight-inch forward out of Southeastern Oklahoma State won seven straight NBA rebounding crowns while splitting time between the Detroit Pistons, San Antonio Spurs, and Chicago Bulls. The only other players in league history with three or more titles have been centers Wilt Chamberlain (eleven), Moses Malone (six), and Bill Russell (four). Part of Rodman's rebounding success must be attributed to his agility. "Most guys are straight-up jumpers," explained broadcaster and former NBA player and coach Johnny Kerr, "but Dennis can adjust his body in the air. The only other player I've seen who could do that was Russell."[44]

Rodman's antics on and off the court got him more than his fair share of headlines and publicity. Technical fouls, fines, and suspensions were all part of the package. So, too, were NBA titles. "The Worm," so-called because of the way he squirmed while playing pinball when he was younger, won a pair of championship rings as a member of the Pistons (1989 and 1990), then three more with Jordan's Bulls (1996, 1997, and 1998).

Added to Rodman's rebounding savvy was a relentless drive and tenacity. He was a member of the NBA All-Defensive First Team seven times, and the league's Defensive Player of the Year twice (1990 and 1991).

Although Michael Jordan has retired, there is no shortage of young stars ready to lead the NBA into the new millennium. As it has in the past, the game will have to adapt to changing conditions. How it does will determine whether or not it maintains its standing as the favorite sport of millions of fans the world over.

Basketball in the Twenty-First Century

WERE JAMES NAISMITH to attend an NBA game in the year 2000, he might have a hard time recognizing his creation. His idea for a recreational activity that would retain the interest of the young men in his class has blossomed in ways he could never have imagined. The basic elements of shooting, rebounding, and passing remain the same, but today's larger, better-conditioned athletes have helped take them to the next level. It is hard to imagine fans today being satisfied with two-handed set shots and jump balls after every basket. For better or worse, the behind-the-back pass, 3-point shot, and slam dunk are here to stay.

Women have become more active in basketball than in other major team sports. The Women's National Basketball Associa-

tion, which began play in 1997, has won over many fans who appreciate the "below-the-rim" game played by the women. Referring to this style of play, all-time great Nancy Lieberman-Cline said, "We work on fundamental skills. . . . Our game is execution because we're not going to overwhelm anybody with physicality."[45] Marketing has made Cynthia Cooper, Teresa Weatherspoon, Lisa Leslie, and others recognizable names on sports pages across the country. Women have also made inroads in a nonplaying capacity. In 1997, Violet Palmer and Dee Kantner became the first women to referee NBA games.

More and more athletes have come to the United States to test their skills against the best basketball players in the world. Players from dozens of foreign lands dot the rosters of major college teams. Sarunas Marciulionis (USSR), Hakeem Olajuwon (Nigeria), Dikembe Mutombo (Zaire), and Toni Kukoc (Yugoslavia) are just four of those who have gone on to enjoy successful careers in the NBA.

Despite—or perhaps because of—its phenomenal growth, basketball has several problems which must be addressed. Trash-talking between players, common in schoolyard games, has become the norm in the pros. Such talk often leads to confrontations on the court, which sometimes result in violence.

Athletes with above-average abilities are treated differently from the time their talents are first noticed. High school and college players often receive special treatment and are not held accountable for their actions. This can lead to irresponsible behavior in later years, with players feeling they do not have to follow the rules that apply to everyone else. Drug usage is just one way in which this behavior may manifest itself. It has been a while since sportscaster Art Rust said, "If cocaine were helium, the whole NBA would float away,"[46] but the danger must never be minimized. All sports must continue the ongoing job of educating players

and making them aware of their standing as role models to youngsters all around the world.

Until recently, basketball could boast of being the only major team sport never to have lost a game due to work stoppage. That streak ended in 1998, when a 191-day strike threatened the season. A settlement negotiated by NBA Commissioner David Stern and Billy Hunter, executive director

Women's National Basketball Association star Cynthia Cooper.

of the players' association, resolved matters before the season had to be canceled.

Recent years have seen more and more college undergraduates try to make the jump to the NBA. The result has affected not only the pro game but the college game as well. Universities can no longer be certain of retaining a star recruit for three or four seasons, as many players apply for the NBA draft after their freshman or sophomore year. This constant turnover has brought a measure of parity to college basketball. North Carolina's Duke University, under coach Mike Krzyzewski, was the only school to maintain its standing at the highest level of the sport throughout the decade of the 1990s.

In spite of these problems, basketball faces the new century with high hopes for further success.

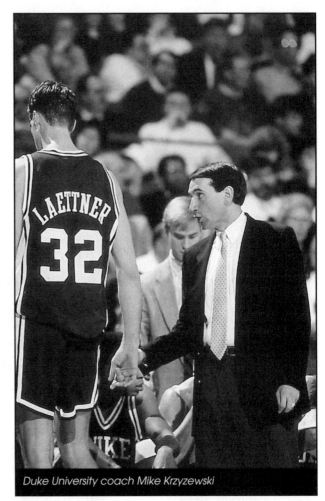

Duke University coach Mike Krzyzewski

The NCAA tournament has become one of sports' biggest events, with the championship contest sure to draw extraordinary television ratings. Basketball has never been more popular with young and old alike. As long as there are driveways and schoolyards where kids can gather to play, the game will continue to grow. Many share the feelings once expressed by coach Lee Rose of the University of North Carolina at Charlotte. "I would like to deny the statement that I think basketball is a matter of life and death," said Rose. "I feel it's much more important than that."[47]

Awards and Statistics

National Champions

The Helms Foundation of Los Angeles, under the direction of founder Bill Schroeder, selected national college basketball champions from 1942 to 1982 and researched retroactive picks from 1901 to 1941. The first NIT tournament and then the NCAA tournament have settled the national championship since 1938, but there are four years (1939, '40, '44, and '54) where the Helms selections differ.

Multiple champions (1901–1937): Chicago, Columbia, and Wisconsin (3); Kansas, Minnesota, Notre Dame, Penn, Pittsburgh, Syracuse, and Yale (2). **Multiple champions (since 1938):** UCLA (11); Kentucky (7); Indiana (5); North Carolina (3); Cincinnati, Duke, Kansas, Louisville, North Carolina State, Oklahoma A&M (now Oklahoma State), and San Francisco (2).

Year	Winner		Head Coach
2000	Michigan State	NCAA	Tom Izzo
1999	Connecticut	NCAA	Jim Calhoun
1998	Kentucky	NCAA	Tubby Smith
1997	Arizona	NCAA	Lute Olson
1996	Kentucky	NCAA	Rick Pitino
1995	UCLA	NCAA	Jim Harrick
1994	Arkansas	NCAA	Nolan Richardson
1993	North Carolina	NCAA	Dean Smith
1992	Duke	NCAA	Mike Krzyzewski
1991	Duke	NCAA	Mike Krzyzewski
1990	UNLV	NCAA	Jerry Tarkanian
1989	Michigan	NCAA	Steve Fisher
1988	Kansas	NCAA	Larry Brown
1987	Indiana	NCAA	Bob Knight
1986	Louisville	NCAA	Denny Crum
1985	Villanova	NCAA	Rollie Massimino
1984	Georgetown	NCAA	John Thompson
1983	N.C. State	NCAA	Jim Valvano
1982	North Carolina	NCAA	Dean Smith

Year	Winner		Head Coach
1981	Indiana	NCAA	Bob Knight
1980	Louisville	NCAA	Denny Crum
1979	Michigan State	NCAA	Jud Heathcote
1978	Kentucky	NCAA	Joe B. Hall
1977	Marquette	NCAA	Al McGuire
1976	Indiana	NCAA	Bob Knight
1975	UCLA	NCAA	John Wooden
1974	N.C. State	NCAA	Norm Sloan
1973	UCLA	NCAA	John Wooden
1972	UCLA	NCAA	John Wooden
1971	UCLA	NCAA	John Wooden
1970	UCLA	NCAA	John Wooden
1969	UCLA	NCAA	John Wooden
1968	UCLA	NCAA	John Wooden
1967	UCLA	NCAA	John Wooden
1966	Texas Western	NCAA	Don Haskins
1965	UCLA	NCAA	John Wooden
1964	UCLA	NCAA	John Wooden
1963	Loyola-IL	NCAA	George Ireland
1962	Cincinnati	NCAA	Ed Jucker
1961	Cincinnati	NCAA	Ed Jucker
1960	Ohio State	NCAA	Fred Taylor
1959	California	NCAA	Pete Newell
1958	Kentucky	NCAA	Adolph Rupp
1957	North Carolina	NCAA	Frank McGuire
1956	San Francisco	NCAA	Phil Woolpert
1955	San Francisco	NCAA	Phil Woolpert
1954	La Salle &	NCAA	Ken Loeffler
	Kentucky (Helms)		Adolph Rupp
1953	Indiana	NCAA	Branch McCracken
1952	Kansas	NCAA	Phog Allen
1951	Kentucky	NCAA	Adolph Rupp
1950	CCNY	NCAA & NIT	Nat Holman
1949	Kentucky	NCAA	Adolph Rupp
1948	Kentucky	NCAA	Adolph Rupp
1947	Holy Cross	NCAA	Doggie Julian

Year	Winner		Head Coach
1946	Oklahoma A&M	NCAA	Hank Iba
1945	Oklahoma A&M	NCAA	Hank Iba
1944	Utah &	NCAA	Vadal Peterson
	Army (Helms)		Ed Kelleher
1943	Wyoming	NCAA	Everett Shelton
1942	Stanford	NCAA	Everett Dean
1941	Wisconsin	NCAA	Bud Foster
1940	Indiana &	NCAA	Branch McCracken
	USC (Helms)		Sam Barry
1939	Oregon &	NCAA	Howard Hobson
	LIU-Brooklyn		
	(Helms)	NIT	Clair Bee
1938	Temple	NIT	James Usilton
1937	Stanford		John Bunn
1936	Notre Dame		George Keogan
1935	NYU		Howard Cann
1934	Wyoming		Willard Witte
1933	Kentucky		Adolph Rupp
1932	Purdue		Piggy Lambert
1931	Northwestern		Dutch Lonborg
1930	Pittsburgh		Doc Carlson
1929	Montana State		Schubert Dyche
1928	Pittsburgh		Doc Carlson
1927	Notre Dame		George Keogan
1926	Syracuse		Lew Andreas
1925	Princeton		Al Wittmer
1924	North Carolina		Bo Shepard
1923	Kansas		Phog Allen
1922	Kansas		Phog Allen
1921	Penn		Edward McNichol
1920	Penn		Lon Jourdet
1919	Minnesota		Louis Cooke
1918	Syracuse		Edmund Dollard
1917	Washington State		Doc Bohler
1916	Wisconsin		Doc Meanwell
1915	Illinois		Ralph Jones
1914	Wisconsin		Doc Meanwell
1913	Navy		Louis Wenzell
1912	Wisconsin		Doc Meanwell
1911	St. John's-NY		Claude Allen
1910	Columbia		Harry Fisher
1909	Chicago		Joseph Raycroft
1908	Chicago		Joseph Raycroft
1907	Chicago		Joseph Raycroft
1906	Dartmouth		No Coach
1905	Columbia		No Coach
1904	Columbia		No Coach
1903	Yale		W. H. Murphy
1902	Minnesota		Louis Cooke
1901	Yale		No Coach

Annual NCAA Division I Scoring Leaders

The NCAA did not begin keeping individual scoring records until the 1947–1948 season. All averages include postseason games where applicable.

Multiple winners: Pete Maravich and Oscar Robertson (3); Darrel Floyd, Charles Jones, Harry Kelly, Frank Selvy and Freeman Williams (2).

Year		Gm.	Pts.	Avg.
2000	Courtney Alexander, Fresno State	27	669	24.8
1999	Alvin Young, Niagara	29	728	25.1
1998	Charles Jones, LIU-Brooklyn	30	869	29.0
1997	Charles Jones, LIU-Brooklyn	30	903	30.1
1996	Kevin Granger, Texas Southern	24	648	27.0
1995	Kurt Thomas, TCU	27	781	28.9
1994	Glenn Robinson, Purdue	34	1030	30.3
1993	Greg Guy, Texas-Pan Am	19	556	29.3
1992	Brett Roberts, Morehead State	29	815	28.1
1991	Kevin Bradshaw, US Int'l	28	1054	37.6
1990	Bo Kimble, Loyola-CA	32	1131	35.3
1989	Hank Gathers, Loyola-CA	31	1015	32.7
1988	Hersey Hawkins, Bradley	31	1125	36.3
1987	Kevin Houston, Army	29	953	32.9
1986	Terrance Bailey, Wagner	29	854	29.4
1985	Xavier McDaniel, Wichita State	31	844	27.2
1984	Joe Jakubick, Akron	27	814	30.1
1983	Harry Kelly, Texas Southern	29	835	28.8
1982	Harry Kelly, Texas Southern	29	862	29.7
1981	Zam Fredrick, S. Carolina	27	781	28.9
1980	Tony Murphy, Southern-BR	29	932	32.1
1979	Lawrence Butler, Idaho State	27	812	30.1
1978	Freeman Williams, Portland State	27	969	35.9
1977	Freeman Williams, Portland State	26	1010	38.8
1976	Marshall Rodgers, Texas-Pan Am	25	919	36.8
1975	Bob McCurdy, Richmond	26	855	32.9
1974	Larry Fogle, Canisius	25	835	33.4
1973	Bird Averitt, Pepperdine	25	848	33.9
1972	Dwight Lamar, SW La	29	1054	36.3
1971	Johnny Neumann, Ole Miss	23	923	40.1

Year		Gm.	Pts.	Avg.	Year		Gm.	Pts.	Avg.
1970	Pete Maravich, LSU	31	1381	44.5	1959	Oscar Robertson, Cincinnati	30	978	32.6
1969	Pete Maravich, LSU	26	1148	44.2	1958	Oscar Robertson, Cincinnati	28	984	35.1
1968	Pete Maravich, LSU	26	1138	43.8	1957	Grady Wallace, S. Carolina	29	906	31.2
1967	Jimmy Walker, Providence	28	851	30.4	1956	Darrell Floyd, Furman	28	946	33.8
1966	Dave Schellhase, Purdue	24	781	32.5	1955	Darrell Floyd, Furman	25	897	35.9
1965	Rick Barry, Miami-FL	26	973	37.4	1954	Frank Selvy, Furman	29	1209	41.7
1964	Howie Komives,				1953	Frank Selvy, Furman	25	738	29.5
	Bowling Green	23	844	36.7	1952	Clyde Lovellette, Kansas	28	795	28.4
1963	Nick Werkman, Seton Hall	22	650	29.5	1951	Bill Mlkvy, Temple	25	731	29.2
1962	Billy McGill, Utah	26	1009	38.8	1950	Paul Arizin, Villanova	29	735	25.3
1961	Frank Burgess, Gonzaga	26	842	32.4	1949	Tony Lavelli, Yale	30	671	22.4
1960	Oscar Robertson, Cincinnati	30	1011	33.7	1948	Murray Wier, Iowa	19	399	21.0

The NBA Finals

Although the National Basketball Association traces its first championship back to the 1946–1947 season, the league was then called the Basketball Association of America (BAA). It did not become the NBA until after the 1948–1949 season when the BAA and the National Basketball League (NBL) agreed to merge.

In the chart below, the Eastern finalists (representing the NBA Eastern Division from 1947–1970, and the NBA Eastern Conference since 1971) are listed in CAPITAL letters.

Multiple winners: Boston (16); Minneapolis/LA Lakers (11); Chicago Bulls (6); Philadelphia/San Francisco Golden State Warriors and Syracuse Nationals/Philadelphia 76ers (3); Detroit, Houston, and New York (2).

Year	Winner	Head Coach	Series	Loser
2000	Los Angeles Lakers	Phil Jackson	4–2	INDIANA PACERS
1999	San Antonio Spurs	Gregg Popovich	4–1	NEW YORK KNICKS
1998	CHICAGO	Phil Jackson	4–2	Utah
1997	CHICAGO	Phil Jackson	4–2	Utah
1996	CHICAGO	Phil Jackson	4–2	Seattle
1995	Houston	Rudy Tomjanovich	4–0	ORLANDO
1994	Houston	Rudy Tomjanovich	4–3	NEW YORK
1993	CHICAGO	Phil Jackson	4–2	Phoenix
1992	CHICAGO	Phil Jackson	4–2	Portland
1991	CHICAGO	Phil Jackson	4–1	LA Lakers
1990	DETROIT PISTONS	Chuck Daly	4–1	Portland
1989	DETROIT PISTONS	Chuck Daly	4–0	LA Lakers
1988	LA Lakers	Pat Riley	4–3	DETROIT PISTONS
1987	LA Lakers	Pat Riley	4–2	BOSTON
1986	BOSTON	K. C. Jones	4–2	Houston
1985	LA Lakers	Pat Riley	4–2	BOSTON
1984	BOSTON	K. C. Jones	4–3	LA Lakers
1983	PHILADELPHIA 76ERS	Billy Cunningham	4–0	LA Lakers
1982	LA Lakers	Pat Riley	4–2	PHILA. 76ERS
1981	BOSTON	Bill Fitch	4–2	Houston
1980	LA Lakers	Paul Westhead	4–2	PHILA. 76ERS
1979	Seattle	Lenny Wilkens	4–1	WASH. BULLETS
1978	WASHINGTON BULLETS	Dick Motta	4–3	Seattle
1977	Portland	Jack Ramsay	4–2	PHILA. 76ERS
1976	BOSTON	Tommy Heinsohn	4–2	Phoenix
1975	Golden State Warriors	Al Attles	4–0	WASH. BULLETS

Year	Winner	Head Coach	Series	Loser
1974	BOSTON	Tommy Heinsohn	4–3	Milwaukee
1973	NEW YORK	Red Holzman	4–1	LA Lakers
1972	LA Lakers	Bill Sharman	4–1	NEW YORK
1971	Milwaukee	Larry Costello	4–0	BALT. BULLETS
1970	NEW YORK	Red Holzman	4–3	LA Lakers
1969	BOSTON	Bill Russell	4–3	LA Lakers
1968	BOSTON	Bill Russell	4–2	LA Lakers
1967	PHILADELPHIA 76ERS	Alex Hannum	4–2	SF Warriors
1966	BOSTON	Red Auerbach	4–3	LA Lakers
1965	BOSTON	Red Auerbach	4–1	LA Lakers
1964	BOSTON	Red Auerbach	4–1	SF Warriors
1963	BOSTON	Red Auerbach	4–2	LA Lakers
1962	BOSTON	Red Auerbach	4–3	LA Lakers
1961	BOSTON	Red Auerbach	4–1	St. Louis Hawks
1960	BOSTON	Red Auerbach	4–3	St. Louis Hawks
1959	BOSTON	Red Auerbach	4–0	Mpls. Lakers
1958	St. Louis Hawks	Alex Hannum	4–2	BOSTON
1957	BOSTON	Red Auerbach	4–3	St. Louis Hawks
1956	PHILADELPHIA WARRIORS	George Senesky	4–1	Ft. Wayne Pistons
1955	SYRACUSE	Al Cervi	4–3	Ft. Wayne Pistons
1954	Minneapolis Lakers	John Kundla	4–3	SYRACUSE
1953	Minneapolis Lakers	John Kundla	4–1	NEW YORK
1952	Minneapolis Lakers	John Kundla	4–3	NEW YORK
1951	Rochester	Les Harrison	4–3	NEW YORK
1950	Minneapolis Lakers	John Kundla	4–2	SYRACUSE
1949	Minneapolis Lakers	John Kundla	4–2	WASH. CAPITOLS
1948	Baltimore Bullets	Buddy Jeannette	4–2	PHILA. WARRIORS
1947	PHILADELPHIA WARRIORS	Eddie Gottlieb	4–1	Chicago Stags

Annual NBA Scoring Leaders

Decided by total points from 1947 to 1969, and per game average since 1970.

Multiple winners: Michael Jordan (10); Wilt Chamberlain (7); George Gervin (4); Neil Johnston, Bob McAdoo, and George Mikan (3); Kareem Abdul-Jabbar, Paul Arizin, Adrian Dantley, and Bob Pettit (2).

Year		Gm.	Pts.	Avg.
2000	Shaquille O'Neal, LA	79	2344	29.7
1999	Allen Iverson, Phil.	48	1284	26.8
1998	Michael Jordan, Chicago	82	2357	28.7
1997	Michael Jordan, Chicago	82	2431	29.7
1996	Michael Jordan, Chicago	82	2491	30.4
1995	Shaquille O'Neal, Orlando	79	2315	29.3
1994	David Robinson, SA	80	2383	29.8
1993	Michael Jordan, Chicago	78	2541	32.6
1992	Michael Jordan, Chicago	80	2404	30.1

Year		Gm.	Pts.	Avg.
1991	Michael Jordan, Chicago	82	2580	31.5
1990	Michael Jordan, Chicago	82	2753	33.6
1989	Michael Jordan, Chicago	81	2633	32.5
1988	Michael Jordan, Chicago	82	2868	35.0
1987	Michael Jordan, Chicago	82	3041	37.1
1986	Dominique Wilkins, Atlanta	78	2366	30.3
1985	Bernard King, NY	55	1809	32.9
1984	Adrian Dantley, Utah	79	2418	30.6
1983	Alex English, Denver	82	2326	28.4
1982	George Gervin, SA	79	2551	32.3
1981	Adrian Dantley, Utah	80	2452	30.7
1980	George Gervin, SA	78	2585	33.1
1979	George Gervin, SA	80	2365	29.6
1978	George Gervin, SA	82	2232	27.2
1977	Pete Maravich, NO	73	2273	31.1
1976	Bob McAdoo, Buffalo	78	2427	31.1
1975	Bob McAdoo, Buffalo	82	2831	34.5

Year		Gm.	Pts.	Avg.
1974	Bob McAdoo, Buffalo	74	2261	30.6
1973	Nate Archibald, KC-Omaha	80	2719	34.0
1972	Kareem Abdul-Jabbar, Milwaukee	81	2822	34.8
1971	Lew Alcindor, Milwaukee	82	2596	31.7
1970	Jerry West, LA	74	2309	31.2
1969	Elvin Hayes, SD	82	2327	28.4
1968	Dave Bing, Detroit	79	2142	27.1
1967	Rick Barry, SF	78	2775	35.6
1966	Wilt Chamberlain, Phil.	79	2649	33.5
1965	Wilt Chamberlain, SF-Phil.	73	2534	34.7
1964	Wilt Chamberlain, SF	80	2948	36.9
1963	Wilt Chamberlain, SF	80	3586	44.8
1962	Wilt Chamberlain, Phil.	80	4029	50.4
1961	Wilt Chamberlain, Phil.	79	3033	38.4
1960	Wilt Chamberlain, Phil.	72	2707	37.6
1959	Bob Pettit, St. Louis	72	2105	29.2
1958	George Yardley, Detroit	72	2001	27.8
1957	Paul Arizin, Phil.	71	1817	25.6
1956	Bob Pettit, St. Louis	72	1849	25.7
1955	Neil Johnston, Phil.	72	1631	22.7
1954	Neil Johnston, Phil.	72	1759	24.4
1953	Neil Johnston, Phil.	70	1564	22.3
1952	Paul Arizin, Phil.	66	1674	25.4
1951	George Mikan, Mpls.	68	1932	28.4
1950	George Mikan, Mpls.	68	1865	27.4
1949	George Mikan, Mpls.	60	1698	28.3
1948	Max Zaslofsky, Chicago	48	1007	21.0
1947	Joe Fulks, Phil.	60	1389	23.2

Most Valuable Player

The Maurice Podoloff Trophy for regular season MVP. Named after the first commissioner (then president) of the NBA. Winners first selected by the NBA players (1956–1980) then a national panel of pro basketball writers and broadcasters (since 1981). Winners' scoring averages are provided; * indicates led league.

Multiple winners: Kareem Abdul-Jabbar (6); Michael Jordan and Bill Russell (5); Wilt Chamberlain (4); Larry Bird, Magic Johnson, and Moses Malone (3); Bob Pettit (2).

Year		Avg.
2000	Shaquille O'Neal, LA, C	29.7

Year		Avg.
1999	Karl Malone, Utah, F	23.8
1998	Michael Jordon, Chicago, G	28.7*
1997	Karl Malone, Utah, F	27.4
1996	Michael Jordan, Chicago G	30.4*
1995	David Robinson, San Antonio, C	27.6
1994	Hakeem Olajuwan, Houston, C	27.3
1993	Charles Barkley, Phoenix, F	25.6
1992	Michael Jordan, Chicago, G	30.1*
1991	Michael Jordan, Chicago, G	31.5*
1990	Magic Johnson, LA, G	22.3
1989	Magic Johnson, LA, G	22.5
1988	Michael Jordan, Chicago, G	35.0*
1987	Magic Johnson, LA, G	23.9
1986	Larry Bird, Boston, F	25.8
1985	Larry Bird, Boston, F	28.7
1984	Larry Bird, Boston, F	24.2
1983	Moses Malone, Philadelphia, C	24.5
1982	Moses Malone, Houston, C	31.1
1981	Julius Erving, Philadelphia, F	24.6
1980	Kareem Abdul-Jabbar, LA, C	24.8
1979	Moses Malone, Houston, C	24.8
1978	Bill Walton, Portland, C	18.9
1977	Kareem Abdul-Jabbar, LA, C	26.2
1976	Kareem Abdul-Jabbar, LA, C	27.7
1975	Bob McAdoo, Buffalo, F	34.5*
1974	Kareem Abdul-Jabbar, LA, C	27.0
1973	Dave Cowens, Boston, C	20.5
1972	Kareem Abdul-Jabbar, Milwaukee, C	34.8*
1971	Lew Alcindor, Milwaukee, C	31.7*
1970	Willis Reed, New York, C	21.7
1969	Wes Unseld, Baltimore, C	13.8
1968	Wilt Chamberlain, Philadelphia, C	24.3
1967	Wilt Chamberlain, Philadelphia, C	24.1
1966	Wilt Chamberlain, Philadelphia, C	33.5*
1965	Bill Russell, Boston, C	14.1
1964	Oscar Robertson, Cincinnati, G	31.4
1963	Bill Russell, Boston, C	16.8
1962	Bill Russell, Boston, C	18.9
1961	Bill Russell, Boston, C	16.9
1960	Wilt Chamberlain, Philadelphia, C	37.6*
1959	Bob Pettit, St. Louis, F	29.2*
1958	Bill Russell, Boston, C	16.6
1957	Bob Cousy, Boston, G	20.6
1956	Bob Pettit, St. Louis, F	25.7*

Rookie of the Year

The Eddie Gottlieb Trophy for outstanding rookie of the regular season. Named after the pro basketball pioneer and owner-coach of the first NBA champion Philadelphia Warriors. Winners selected by a national panel of pro basketball writers and broadcasters. Winners' scoring averages provided; * indicated led league; winners who were also named MVP are in **bold** type.

Year		Avg.
2000	Elton Brand, Chicago, F	20.1
	& Steve Francis, Houston, G	18.0
1999	Vince Carter, Toronto, G	18.3
1998	Tim Duncan, San Antonio, F/C	21.6
1997	Allen Iverson, Philadelphia, G	23.5
1996	Damon Stoudamire, Toronto, G	19.0
1995	Grant Hill, Detroit, F	19.9
	& Jason Kidd, Dallas, G	11.7
1994	Chris Webber, Golden St., F	17.5
1993	Shaquille O'Neal, Orlando, C	23.4
1992	Larry Johnson, Charlotte, F	19.2
1991	Derrick Coleman, New Jersey, F	18.4
1990	David Robinson, San Antonio, C	24.3
1989	Mitch Richmond, Golden St., G	22.0
1988	Mark Jackson, New York, G	13.6
1987	Chuck Person, Indiana, F	18.8
1986	Patrick Ewing, New York, C	20.0
1985	Michael Jordan, Chicago, G	28.2
1984	Ralph Sampson, Houston, C	21.0
1983	Terry Cummings, San Diego, F	23.7
1982	Buck Williams, New Jersey, F	15.5
1981	Darrell Griffith, Utah, G	20.6
1980	Larry Bird, Boston, F	21.3
1979	Phil Ford, Kansas City, G	15.9
1978	Walter Davis, Phoenix, G	24.2
1977	Adrian Dantley, Buffalo, F	20.3
1976	Alvan Adams, Phoenix, C	19.0
1975	Keith Wilkes, Golden St., F	14.2
1974	Ernie DiGregorio, Buffalo, G	15.2
1973	Bob McAdoo, Buffalo, C/F	18.0
1972	Sidney Wicks, Portland, F	24.5
1971	Dave Cowens, Boston, C	17.0
	& Geoff Petrie, Portland, G	24.8
1970	Lew Alcindor, Milwaukee Bucks, C	28.8
1969	**Wes Unseld**, Baltimore, C	13.8
1968	Earl Monroe, Baltimore, G	24.3
1967	Dave Bing, Detroit, G	20.0
1966	Rick Barry, San Francisco, F	25.7

Year		Avg.
1965	Willis Reed, New York, C	19.5
1964	Jerry Lucas, Cincinnati, F/C	17.7
1963	Terry Dischinger, Chicago Zephyrs, F	25.5
1962	Walt Bellamy, Chicago Packers, C	31.6
1961	Oscar Robertson, Cincinnati, G	30.5
1960	**Wilt Chamberlain**, Philadelphia, C	37.6*
1959	Elgin Baylor, Minneapolis, F	24.9
1958	Woody Sauldsberry, Philadelphia, F/C	12.8
1957	Tommy Heinsohn, Boston, F	16.2
1956	Maurice Stokes, Rochester, F/C	16.8
1955	Bob Pettit, Milwaukee Hawks, F	20.4
1954	Ray Felix, Baltimore, C	17.6
1953	Don Meineke, Ft. Wayne, F	10.8

Defensive Player of the Year

Awarded to the best defensive player for the regular season. Winners selected by a national panel of pro basketball writers and broadcasters.

Multiple winners: Dikembe Mutombo (3); Mark Eaton, Sidney Moncrief, Alonzo Mourning, Hakeem Olajuwon, and Dennis Rodman (2).

Year	
2000	Alonzo Mourning, Miami, C
1999	Alonzo Mourning, Miami, C
1998	Dikembe Mutombo, Atlanta, C
1997	Dikembe Mutombo, Atlanta,, C
1996	Gary Payton, Seattle, G
1995	Dikembe Mutombo, Denver, C
1994	Hakeem Olajuwon, Houston, C
1993	Hakeem Olajuwon, Houston, C
1992	David Robinson, San Antonio, C
1991	Dennis Rodman, Detroit, F
1990	Dennis Rodman, Detroit, F
1989	Mark Eaton, Utah, C
1988	Michael Jordan, Chicago, G
1987	Michael Cooper, LA Lakers, F
1986	Alvin Robertson, San Antonio, G
1985	Mark Eaton, Utah, C
1984	Sidney Moncrief, Milwaukee, G
1983	Sidney Moncrief, Milwaukee, G

Notes

Introduction: A Worldwide Mania

1. Quoted in Alexander Wolff, *Basketball: A History of the Game.* New York: Time, 1997, p. 7.

Chapter 1: From Humble Beginnings

2. Quoted in Wolff, *Basketball: A History of the Game,* p. 8.
3. James Naismith, *Basketball: Its Origin and Development.* Lincoln: University of Nebraska Press, 1996, p. 33.
4. Quoted in Wolff, *Basketball: A History of the Game,* p. 8.
5. Quoted in Basketball Hall of Fame history section, www.hoophall.com/hoophistory/naismith.cfm.
6. Naismith, *Basketball: Its Origin and Development,* pp. 53–55.
7. Naismith, *Basketball: Its Origin and Development,* p. 56.
8. Quoted in Robert W. Peterson, *Cages to Jump Shots.* New York: Oxford University Press, 1990, p. 28.

Chapter 2: The Evolution of a Simple Game

9. Naismith, *Basketball: Its Origin and Development,* p. 86.
10. Quoted in Peterson, *Cages to Jump Shots,* p. 37.

Chapter 3: The Pros Come of Age

11. Quoted in Zander Hollander, ed., *The NBA's Official Encyclopedia of Pro Basketball.* New York: New American Library, 1981, p. 3.
12. Quoted in Peter C. Bjarkman, *The Biographical History of Basketball.* Chicago: Masters Press, 2000, p. 261.
13. Quoted in Peterson, *Cages to Jump Shots,* p. 33.
14. Quoted in Zander Hollander and Alex Sachare, eds., *The Official NBA Basketball Encyclopedia.* New York: Villard Books, 1989, p. 16.
15. Quoted in Hollander and Sachare, *The Official NBA Basketball Encyclopedia,* p. 18.

16. Quoted in Peterson, *Cages to Jump Shots,* p. 81.
17. Quoted in Bjarkman, *The Biographical History of Basketball,* p. 219.
18. Quoted in Vincent M. Mallozzi, *Basketball: The Legends and the Game.* Buffalo, NY: Firefly Books, 1998, p. 16.
19. Quoted in Hollander and Sachare, *The Official NBA Basketball Encyclopedia,* p. 28.
20. Quoted in Mallozzi, *Basketball: The Legends and the Game,* p. 146.
21. Quoted in Peterson, *Cages to Jump Shots,* p. 109.
22. Quoted in Wolff, *Basketball: A History of the Game,* p. 98.
23. Quoted in Dave Anderson, *The History of Basketball.* New York: William Morrow, 1997, pp. 33–34.
24. Quoted in Jim Savage, *The Encyclopedia of the NCAA Basketball Tournament.* New York: Dell, 1990, p. 4.

Chapter 4: The Modern–Day Game

25. Quoted in Peterson, *Cages to Jump Shots,* p. 125.
26. Quoted in Leonard Koppett, *24 Seconds to Shoot.* 1968. Reprint, Kingston, NY: Total/Sports Illustrated, 1999, p. 59.
27. Quoted in Leigh Montville, "In the Nick of Time," *Sports Illustrated,* November 6, 1989, p. 106.
28. Quoted in Montville, "In the Nick of Time," p. 106.
29. Quoted in Anderson, *The History of Basketball*, p. 75.
30. Quoted in Hollander and Sachare, *The Official NBA Basketball Encyclopedia,* p. 145.
31. Quoted in Wolff, *Basketball: A History of the Game,* p. 130.

Chapter 5: Superstars One and All

32. Quoted in Wolff, *Basketball: A History of the Game,* p. 132.
33. Quoted in Wolff, *Basketball: A History of the Game,* p. 124.
34. Quoted in Bjarkman, *The Biographical History of Basketball,* p. 529.
35. Quoted in Wolff, *Basketball: A History of the Game,* p. 138.
36. Quoted in Mallozzi, *Basketball: The Legends and the Game*, p. 118.
37. Quoted in Zander Hollander, ed. *The Modern Encyclopedia of Basketball.* New York: Four Winds Press, 1973, p. 350.
38. Quoted in Hollander, *The Modern Encyclopedia of Basketball,* p. 329.
39. Quoted in Bjarkman, *The Biographical History of Basketball,* p. 134.
40. Quoted in Wolff, *Basketball: A History of the Game,* p. 120.
41. Quoted in Anderson, *The History of Basketball,* p. 101.

42. Quoted in Wolff, *Basketball: A History of the Game,* p. 128.
43. Quoted in Phil Taylor, "Keep It Simple," *Sports Illustrated,* May 10, 1999, p. 50.
44. Quoted in Anderson, *The History of Basketball,* p. 120.

Epilogue: Basketball in the Twenty–First Century

45. Quoted in Anderson, *The History of Basketball,* p. 138.
46. Quoted in Lee Green, ed., *Sportswit.* New York: Fawcett Crest, 1984, p. 55.
47. Quoted in Green, *Sportswit,* p. 54.

For Further Reading

Books

Pete Axthelm, *The City Game: Basketball from the Garden to the Playgrounds.* New York: Harpers Magazine Press, 1970. Axthelm gives the reader a look into the subculture that is the playground game of basketball.

Bill Bradley, *Life on the Run.* New York: Quadrangle, 1976. The former basketball star and Rhodes scholar presents an inside look at the life of a professional athlete.

Bob Cousy and Frank G. Power Jr., *Basketball Concepts and Techniques.* Boston: Allyn and Bacon, 1970. For coaches, or anyone interested in learning the finer points of the game, this book by Hall of Famer Cousy is an excellent resource.

John Feinstein, *A March to Madness.* Boston: Little, Brown, 1998. This book reveals the hidden world of college basketball in a look at the 1996–1997 Atlantic Coast Conference season.

Sam Goldpaper, *Great Moments in Pro Basketball.* New York: Tempo Books, 1977. The veteran basketball correspondent presents a look at some of the most memorable teams, players, and games in the history of the National Basketball Association.

David Halberstam, *The Breaks of the Game.* New York: Alfred A. Knopf, 1981. The book presents a look at the world of professional basketball as embodied by the 1979–1980 Portland Trail Blazers.

Terry Pluto, *Loose Balls: The Short, Wild Life of the American Basketball Association as Told by the Players, Coaches, and Movers and Shakers Who Made It Happen.* New York: Simon and Schuster, 1990. This book presents an in-depth look at the life and times of the upstart American Basketball Association.

Charles Salzberg, ed., *From Set Shot to Slam Dunk: The Glory Days of Basketball in the Words of Those Who Played It.* New York: E. P. Dutton, 1987. Former players reminisce about the early days of the National Basketball Association.

Dave Zinkoff and Edgar Williams, *Go, Man, Go!* New York: Pyramid Books, 1958. This book details the often hilarious history of basketball's clown princes, the Harlem Globetrotters.

Websites

Basketball Hall of Fame (www.hoophall.com/index.cfm). This is the official website of the Basketball Hall of Fame in Springfield, Massachusetts.

Continental Basketball Association (www.cbahoops.com). This is the official website of the Continental Basketball Association.

National Basketball Association (www.nba.com). This is the official website of the National Basketball Association.

Works Consulted

Books

Dave Anderson, *The History of Basketball.* New York: William Morrow, 1997. An entertaining history of basketball, with an excellent section detailing the fundamentals of the game.

————, *The Story of Football.* New York: Beech Tree Paperback Book, 1997. An updated version of this author's 1985 history of the game.

Peter C. Bjarkman, *The Biographical History of Basketball.* Chicago: Masters Press, 2000. A fascinating look at the history of basketball through the biographies of more than five hundred of the game's most famous and significant personalities.

Gene Brown, ed., *The New York Times Encyclopedia of Sports: Basketball.* New York: Arno Press, 1979. This volume is a collection of articles from the *New York Times* tracing the history of basketball from 1897 to 1979.

Lee Green, ed., *Sportswit.* New York: Fawcett Crest, 1984. A collection of sports quotes on a variety of subjects.

Zander Hollander, ed., *The Modern Encyclopedia of Basketball.* New York: Four Winds Press, 1973. In addition to the usual statistics, this encyclopedia includes biographies of many college and professional greats.

————, *The NBA's Official Encyclopedia of Pro Basketball.* New York: New American Library, 1981. An early encyclopedia which includes complete yearly summaries of each NBA season and All-Star Games, as well as statistical data on each NBA player.

Zander Hollander and Alex Sachare, eds., *The Official NBA Basketball Encyclopedia.* New York: Villard Books, 1989. This volume contains complete statistical records for every player to appear in an NBA game.

Neil D. Isaacs, *All the Moves.* New York: Harper Colophon Books, 1984. A history of college basketball from its birth up through the 1980s.

Leonard Koppett, *24 Seconds to Shoot*. 1968. Reprint, Kingston, NY: Total/Sports Illustrated, 1999. This book details the history of the National Basketball Association from its beginning through 1968.

Vincent M. Mallozzi, *Basketball: The Legends and the Game*. Buffalo, NY: Firefly Books, 1998. This lavishly illustrated volume pays tribute to three hundred of the greatest athletes to ever play the game.

Ronald L. Mendell, *Who's Who in Basketball*. New Rochelle, NY: Arlington House, 1973. This volume contains profiles of more than nine hundred basketball personalities from the game's birth in 1891 through 1973.

James Naismith, *Basketball: Its Origin and Development*. Lincoln: University of Nebraska Press, 1996. This reprint of the 1941 book contains thoughts on the creation of basketball by the game's inventor, as well as a new introduction by a University of Maine history professor.

Robert W. Peterson, *Cages to Jump Shots*. New York: Oxford University Press, 1990. This book examines the early years of the game, up through the first years of the NBA. Of special note is a detailed appendix listing the standings of the major professional leagues from 1898 to 1954.

Charles Salzberg, *From Set Shot to Slam Dunk*. New York: E. P. Dutton, 1987. A look at basketball through the 1940s, '50s, and '60s, through the eyes of the men who played it.

Jim Savage, *The Encyclopedia of the NCAA Basketball Tournament*. New York: Dell, 1990. This volume details the complete history of the NCAA tournament from its inception in 1939 through 1990. The book also contains game box scores, records, and biographies of the top players and coaches.

Mark Stewart, *Basketball: A History of Hoops*. New York: Franklin Watts, 1998. This book discusses the origins and evolution of the sport, as well as important events and personalities in its history.

David Wolf, *Foul!* New York: Warner, 1972. This biography of Connie Hawkins traces his life from his early days as a playground legend to his eventual career as an NBA superstar.

Alexander Wolff, *Basketball: A History of the Game*. New York: Time, 1997. This volume in the lavishly illustrated series of *Sports Illustrated* books chronicles the amazing growth of James Naismith's sport.

Periodicals

Michael Bamberger, "Everything You Always Wanted to Know About Free Throws," *Sports Illustrated,* April 13, 1998.

Dave Kindred, "Of Arrogance and Infamy," *Sporting News,* January 18, 1993.

Paul Levy, "In 1891 in Springfield, Mass., Dr. James Naismith Gave the World a New Passion, Basketball," *Sports History,* July 1988.

Leigh Montville, "In the Nick of Time," *Sports Illustrated,* November 6, 1989.

Robert W. Peterson, "When the Court Was a Cage," *Sports Illustrated,* November 11, 1991.

Gary Smith, "A Few Pieces of Silver," *Sports Illustrated,* June 15, 1992.

Phil Taylor, "Keep It Simple," *Sports Illustrated,* May 10, 1999.

Index

Picture Credits

Cover Photo: © Bettmann/Corbis
AP Photo, 11, 42, 64
AP Photo/Gerry Broome, 8
AP Photo/Michael Okoniewski, 49
AP Photo/Orlin Wagner, 23
Basketball Hall of Fame, 20, 21, 27, 30, 32, 34, 35, 38
© Bettmann/Corbis, 16, 50, 53, 55, 60
© Rich Clarkson/Allsport, 76
© Jonathan Daniel/Allsport, 56, 69, 70, 71
© FPG International, 18, 59, 65
© Otto Greule/Allsport, 72
© Charles Harris/Corbis, 36
© Minnesota Historical Society/Corbis, 44
Sporting News/Archive Photos, 47, 61, 63
© Rick Stewart/Focus West/Allsport, 22
© TempSport/Corbis, 13
© Todd Warshaw/Allsport, 75

About the Author

John F. Grabowski is a native of Brooklyn, New York. He holds a bachelor's degree in psychology from City College of New York and a master's degree in educational psychology from Teacher's College, Columbia University. He has been a teacher for thirty-one years, as well as a freelance writer, specializing in the fields of sports, education, and comedy. His body of published work includes twenty-two books; a nationally syndicated sports column; consultation on several math textbooks; articles for newspapers, magazines, and the programs of professional sports teams; and comedy material sold to Jay Leno, Joan Rivers, and numerous other comics. He and his wife, Patricia, live in Staten Island with their daughter, Elizabeth.